LABOR AND
THE PUBLIC INTEREST

W. WILLARD WIRTZ

LABOR AND THE PUBLIC INTEREST

Introduction by John T. Dunlop

HARPER & ROW, PUBLISHERS
NEW YORK, EVANSTON, AND LONDON

All royalties for this book will go to
the John Fitzgerald Kennedy Memorial Library.

FIRST EDITION

1

LIBRARY OF CONGRESS CATALOG CARD NUMBER: 64-25666

I-O

"With your permission, I introduce to you the author, in a very real sense, of these remarks and all you will in the future hear from me: my father."

National Press Club
Washington, September 25, 1962

CONTENTS

PREFACE

One of the rigors of public office is maintaining the constant flow of words it demands, and trying to sustain these utterances with at least a minimum diet of reasonable good sense. The land is covered with organizations given to the habit of weekly, monthly, or annual meetings, all to be addressed by speakers summoned from as great a distance as the organizational treasury permits. While other advanced societies have wisely put the siesta after the noonday meal and reduced after-dinner eloquence to the sensible brevity of the toast, we continue here to nourish the illusion that extended oratory is an aid to digestion. It is part of the code that government officials are fair game for the predatory pursuits of program chairmen, whether their blandishment is a free meal or an honorary doctoral degree.

Despite all this, the pages that follow reflect the satisfaction there has been in trying to say from time to time over the past three years what has come to mind under the pressures of forensic duty—and not really unwillingly at all. For communication is both the most difficult and most critical part of making democracy work. Words are the necessary currency for exchanging the capital of ideas and ideals, and if speeches are a declining and corrupted art form there is nevertheless some purpose in trying to put what seems right and worthwhile in understandable shape—without making it any drearier than the circumstances demand. Even if an audience has relinquished voluntarily its freedom from speech it retains the right, I think, not to be bored. Indeed, as the world gets more complicated it may be less important for its speakers to appeal to their listeners' sense of destiny than to their sense of humor—which is only knowing how to distinguish between what is important and what isn't.

It may also compensate some who are tired of listening to note that even a poor speech has had the value, in its preparation, of putting to the tough test of contemplated exposure some thoughts that might otherwise have stayed in the speaker's mind despite their fatal weakness. I have been appalled sometimes at the realization of having come within a final draft of expressing some idea I had grown fond of but which emerged, when it went onto paper, as naked nonsense.

The items which appear in these pages have no single theme, except as they all relate in one way or another to this riddle of reconciling "public" and "private" interests, especially in the labor field. There are, nevertheless, two more general thoughts that are clearer to me for having put this book together. One is that almost every issue in public affairs reduces to a question of how change is to be dealt with; and particularly whether the fact of change has in itself any elements of goodness or badness. I think it has not: that change is inevitable and opposing it is wrong, but that what change is good and what is bad, and when it is time for it, depends entirely on other measures and values.

The second thought—no newer or more novel than Matthew 7:12—is that both the largest personal satisfaction and the meaning of organized society lie in the individual's opportunity to exercise some kind of helpful influence on other people's lives. If this is only the Golden Rule, and John Donne's no man being an island, and his tolling bell, it is nevertheless an emerging motive force in the increasingly complex and interdependent society. The Peace Corps, the Civil Rights Act, and the "war on poverty" are reflections of the growing influence of the classical personal ethic on democracy's contemporary public philosophy.

There are a few more personal things to be said about the preparation of these speeches and of this volume.

Fairly extensive liberties have been taken in reproducing the items which are included here. Some which were given extemporaneously have been pared down from the transcript form. Others have been shortened to avoid, or at least reduce, repetition; but some repetition remains, less the product of loose editing or infatuation with a phrase than of the feeling that the context seemed to require it. Where there is awkwardness of organization it comes at least in part from a deliberate judgment that there was something to be said for leaving the speech whatever integrity it had—as a speech. In several instances, however, two or three speeches have been telescoped together.

It is conceivable, recognizing the contemporary forensic mores and the occasional cynicism about them, that there may be curiosity about how these words were originally put together. I think they all came from, or at least through, my own pen. But there is as much apology as pride in saying this, for it is a kind of vestigial Puritan ethic that it is virtuous for someone to write his own speeches and indecent to use help on them. The more pragmatic view would be that a public official should be censured for taking time from the discharge of his responsibilities to 190 million people to write a speech for an audience of several hundred. Nor does it lessen the offense, perhaps, that most of this writing was done in the evening—which means the time was stolen from my wife, Jane (who often had to listen to the first drafts and say where they were poor), and from our sons, Dick and Philip.

There are other creditors. None of this would have happened if it hadn't been for Arthur J. Goldberg, whom it was my immeasurable good fortune to have the opportunity to serve, as his Under Secretary of Labor, for two years. It would be presumptuous to more than acknowledge my debt of related but incomparable kind to President John F. Kennedy and to President Lyndon B. Johnson. Years of association with Adlai E. Stevenson create a different, but equally immeasurable, kind of indebtedness.

There are many others, in the Department of Labor, whose ideas—and in some cases whose phrases, and even paragraphs—are here, if in remolded form. This is true especially of Daniel P. Moynihan, Stanley Ruttenberg, Charles Donahue, Edith Cook, James J. Reynolds, John Leslie, Joe Judge, John Donovan, Millard Cass. Helen May and Arlene Huff have typed and retyped draft after draft, often late at night; and so, in the preparation of this book, have Cora Holland and Val Harris.

My most immediate and largest debt is to my associates, N. Thompson Powers and Fred Graham. They insisted that this project was worthwhile, and then proceeded to do in the editing of it much more than this term normally implies. I must hope they will find their satisfaction in sharing whatever is legitimately mine.

I am grateful beyond expression to John Dunlop for his willingness to contribute the Introduction. He has combined the practice and the teaching of labor economics and labor arbitration and constructive bargaining in a way which makes him as large a creditor as these professions have.

W. W. W.

INTRODUCTION

There are giant forces at work in our land reshaping large areas of our private and public lives. They are creating new problems and new opportunities. The more significant of the proximate initiators of change in this decade can be briefly identified:

Population growth. The 1960's are expected to see an increase of almost 30 million Americans. The schools, highways and transport, homes and jobs required for our larger citizenry are a challenge worthy of our heritage as pioneers.

New technology. For the first time in human history substantial resources, $15 billion now and perhaps $30 billion by 1970, are being devoted to research and development. Old products and techniques, old jobs and skills, or old weapons systems face the continuing competition of the new. Technological change is no longer the chance result of the isolated inventor; it is the output of the new and growing industry of discovery.

New international economy. Western Europe and Japan,

after a postwar era of reconstruction and modernization, provide us both keen competition and substantial markets for our industrial output. The newly developing nations look to us for the export of capital, for the training of high-level manpower and for technical know-how. These new international imperatives are reshaping our economy and affecting the operations of our universities, labor unions and business corporations.

Shifts in the work force. The farm and rural locale of our work force continues to decline rapidly. Farm jobs fell from 14.0 to 6.7 percent of total employment in the last decade and a half. The dominance of the urban and metropolitan community is drastically transforming political representation. The West and South continue to grow more rapidly than the rest of the nation. Women constitute an increasing proportion, now one-third, of our labor force, and married women who have raised their families are returning to the labor force with increasing frequency. The two million youths entering the labor force each year in this decade constitute an expanded proportion of the work force.

New incomes and rising expectations. The uncomfortable contrasts between our democratic ideals and economic potential, on the one hand, and the performance of our society for many segments of our people, on the other, are a major initiator of social change. We have enjoyed rapidly increasing living standards in the postwar years. Median family income in real terms rose almost 50 percent since the end of World War II to a level of $6,000 in current prices. But these gains, by contrast, have been compelling attention to the pockets of poverty and the cruel consequences of discrimination, lack of education and poor schooling, illness, disabilities and disadvantage.

This volume is concerned with new policies and relationships designed to cope with the consequences generated by population growth, new technology, new international relations, and the other initiators of change noted above which are also creating new urgencies and require new priorities. The major emphasis is upon the following areas, policies and relationships to meet the needs of this decade:

A new federalism. The increased needs for education, urban development and welfare activities have expanded the role of governments, but the overwhelming proportion of the growth in public employment has taken place at state and local levels. "For every federal worker added since 1947, 9 workers have been added to state or local payrolls." The conventional dichotomy between federal and state or local is inadequate to meet the problems of the times or to describe what has been happening in the cooperation between various levels of government in providing resources and administering new programs.

Education and training for youth. The vast deficiencies in education of many youths, often derived from poverty and discrimination, place programs for education and training at the center of activities designed to meet the plight of the disadvantaged. "Every undereducated, undertrained youth from a poverty background entering our work force today will cost us approximately $30,000 in various kinds of welfare payments in the course of his life. Either we help the youth or we support the adult."

More versatile labor force. In a world of rapid technological change, shifting job requirements and a changing labor force, it is imperative that workers be well trained and that arrangements be made for frequent retraining and acquisition of new skills. "In a properly functioning economy it ought to be possible for even most of the retraining job to be done privately. But we are not at that point today." Investments in retraining, improving labor market information and the mobility of the labor force are requisite to a dynamic economy.

Higher priority on full employment and job creation. Full employment is essential to remedy discrimination and to improve the lot of the disadvantaged. The full utilization of human resources is requisite to achieve the potentials of the individual citizen and the society. "America is in many ways like Gulliver in Lilliput—a giant held down by a mass of small doubts and restrictions, needing only to exert the strength of its convictions to realize its full potentials. The hard truth of the matter is that nothing—nothing!—is needed to put this country on a full employment basis except the decision to do it." ". . . inflation, fiscal irresponsibility and international bankruptcy are vices the economy simply cannot afford. But neither can it afford unemployment . . . it would be a serious error if the country were to become conditioned to the idea that 4 percent would be, for any reason, a satisfactory unemployment rate."

New patterns of labor-management relationships. The problems of the decade require new attitudes and approaches and new methods of collective bargaining which are already beginning to emerge. The public has become less tolerant of strike inconveniences, and in many situations with automated plants and increased technical supervision, the strike is not an effective weapon to induce agreement.

The new joint study committees, such as the Human Relations Committee and Kaiser Plan in basic steel, are helping to reduce the extent of crisis-bargaining and to assist the parties to take long-run views of the complex adjustments required for technological change and new competitive forces in the economy. "This, then, seems the likely future course of collective bargaining if it is to preserve its meaningfulness: that it will take larger account of the responsibilities which the new forces loose in the world have created; that its procedures will continue to develop along new lines which make it a more reasoned sort of process; and that there will be a converging and a coordination of public and private decision-making in the whole area of labor relations. There will be, in short, more reliance in collective bargaining on the principles of government, more use in government of the resources and procedures of collective bargaining, and more coordination of the two processes."

These five areas of private and public policy making involve only some of the major transformations which Secretary Wirtz portrays to cope with the forces let loose in our land by the major initiators of change. He also points to new roles for American labor and management overseas, to new interests of the labor movement in community activities, to new functions required of private and public agencies in the labor market, to new meaning for our ideals of democracy and equality of opportunity, and to new ways of formulating social policy.

Secretary Wirtz not only proposes policy programs designed to meet the new problems created for this decade by the great initiators of change, but these eloquent speeches also articulate the philosophy of a dedicated public official.

Among the most interesting passages are those which consider the public interest and the role of government. ". . . the service of the public interest is simply the pursuit by free minds, strengthened with knowledge, of ultimate values."

In an increasing range of activities, executive agencies are not primarily concerned with regulation or dictation. They are rather initiators and catalysts; they explore possibilities, mediate among conflicting interests, and propose and formulate acceptable terms on which the affected individuals and groups may live together, if not prosper; they seek to keep social friction at tolerable levels. The public interest is not the simple sum of all the private interests, but neither is it necessarily different from the private interests directly involved; nor is there any formula to weight or to adjust seasonally the influence of the various minorities which constitute a community. The public interest is not to be identified with the immediate interest; neither is it the same as that of unborn generations. Aggregate economics or sample surveys have no monopoly in the discernment of the public interest. In the absence of precision in measurement of the public interest, the philosophy of top policy makers is the more decisive. For Secretary Wirtz there are three elements to the individual decision making that democracy depends upon: the free mind, knowing the facts, and commitment to ultimate values.

When the Labor Department was established in 1913 its mandate was "to foster, promote, and develop the welfare of the wage earners of the United States, to improve their working conditions, and to advance their opportunities for profitable employment." A measure of the redefinition and enlargement of these responsibilities in our times is seen in the main policy preoccupations of this volume—equal opportunities, manpower training, full employment, youth and education, collective bargaining, international trade negotiations and automation. The range of activities of Secretary Wirtz is further illustrated in the diversity of audiences before whom these statements and remarks were originally made: Congressional committees, government administrators, labor union conventions, business groups, professional societies, voluntary associations of many interests, university lectures and commencement exercises. We are grateful for this opportunity which now permits all of us to listen in on these stimulating addresses.

JOHN T. DUNLOP

LABOR AND THE PUBLIC INTEREST

I

THE RIDDLE OF THE PUBLIC INTEREST

TWO SETS OF INFLUENCES shape whatever life comes to mean for any of us: those we are born heir to and have no choice about, and those we expose ourselves to by our own choosing—friends, books, and the college we turn to.

I cannot find the way, even now, twenty-nine years later, to say my thanks to Beloit. Perhaps such thanks lie, meaningfully, only in whatever we become, and in our realization of how much the college is of whatever we are. This includes, for me, not only education but wife. As large a debtor on both scores as Beloit will ever have, I speak what is, I know, the gratitude you of this Class of '62 feel today, and will feel increasingly with each passing year.

I propose to talk about a client of mine. Recognizing the general and proper constraint upon lawyers' public discussion of their clients' affairs, this seems, nevertheless, a special case.

This client, enjoying a measure of notoriety, has been

* Beloit College Commencement Exercises, Beloit, Wisconsin, June 3, 1962.

variously, not always charitably, characterized: by Voltaire as "a ferocious beast"; by Hazlitt as "a mean, stupid, dastardly, pitiful, selfish, spiteful, envious, ungrateful animal"; and by D. H. Lawrence as "feeble-minded like an idiot." Such description is unduly harsh. I have, to be sure, found this client difficult in the extreme, of constantly changeable mind, rich beyond measure yet mired deep in debt, magnanimous but miserly, never sure whether to be served or not, and very bad pay indeed. Yet, with all, this is a client so satisfying, in my experience, as to justify representation above all others.

I speak of "the public."

This is a strange relationship, between democracy's principals and its agents. I thought about it the other day in connection with a little incident outside the Washington airport. Coming up to this embarrassingly long, black car that was waiting for me, I encountered a man, a stranger, who had opened the door and was looking in at the dashboard, which is equipped to pilot a jet aircraft across the Atlantic. He was a little embarrassed and said something apologetically about "just admiring your car." "No," I said, "it belongs to you," and then, because he looked blank, "I work for the government." He stood there a moment and then put out his hand. "Funny," he said, "I never thought of it that way."

It is funny. We subscribe proudly and wholeheartedly to what Theodore Parker, the abolitionist preacher, described in 1850, thirteen years before Gettysburg, as "the American idea . . . a democracy,—that is a government of all the people, by all the people, for all the people." Yet our general habit is to consider the government almost as a foreign power, even—especially at tax time—more as enemy than ally. We warn it sharply that it is a government of laws, not men, and that we will feel that it governs best if it governs least.

A series of recent developments have put these aphorisms to new testing.

Labor unions and employers, preparing to exercise traditional rights to make their own settlements in their own way—and on the traditional American assumption, remarked by George Bernard Shaw, that "The answer to all disputes is a punch in the jaw"—have been brought up short with insistent demands that they not disrupt the economy by shutdowns and furthermore that their wage bargains comport with the national interest. A major industry, exercising the ultimate prerogative to raise its prices, has been required to reverse its decisions. Television networks have encountered an imperative demand that they do their programming with other interests than their own in mind.

No new laws have been passed to accomplish these results. In an extraordinary fashion "the public interest" has simply been asserted—effectively—as a significant measure of private responsibility.

If these developments have met generally with approval, they give pause at the same time to those most concerned with democracy's process. For they suggest a shifting of previous assumptions that at least so far as economic affairs are concerned the public interest will be sufficiently and best served by accepting the free interplay of opposing self-interests.

This is partly because of the enlarged power and concentration of the market place forces. With increased power in single units, corporations, or labor unions, to affect by their decisions the affairs of others, there develops inevitably a broader concept of responsibility. It is partly, too, the consequence of a narrowing margin for error, for waste, for loss, in a world committed now and indefinitely to what were previously counted emergency conditions.

But there is a harder question here.

If there is to be price stability without price controls, labor peace without compulsory arbitration, the voluntary substitution of great books for great guns on television, and if the guideline for action is to be an unwritten concept of "the public interest," then there is new need to consider how "the public interest" is to be determined and served.

The phrase itself is virtually meaningless, so often corrupted to cloak the user's self-interest that it has become, standing alone, almost a semantic illusion, the stuff for making speeches, not decisions.

Where, then, is one charged with responsibility for representing "the public interest," or required to respect it, to find the content which makes the standard meaningful?

Twenty years of facing this question should perhaps have supplied at least the elements of answers to it. Yet the more I see of democracy's workings, the less clear I am about the answer to the essential riddle of how the ideas and dreams of millions of individual human beings are transmuted into viable public policy.

You will say, and properly, that so far as the business of government is concerned this is essentially a matter of people electing representatives who pass laws which other officers of government then apply. But this leaves the hard part of it. No law has been written and none will be which does not require that its interstices be filled in through the exercise of human discretion and responsibility. The still harder task, in the exercise of the executive function of government, is to meet the situations where the public demands that its interest be served, but where, in Mr. Justice Holmes' putting of it, "opposite convictions still keep a battle front against each other [and] the time for law has not come."

Arguably, if no law has been passed, there is no executive function of government to be performed. The realities are to the contrary. Yesterday morning's *New York Times* carries ten leading stories involving action taken or proposed by the federal government—regarding such matters as nuclear tests, disarmament, major labor disputes. Seven, and possibly eight, of these ten stories concern matters requiring the exercise of executive responsibility virtually unguided by legislative direction.

I think of the problem of finding the public interest in terms, if you will forgive another personal incident, of a case that was being considered by the War Labor Board at an evening session fairly early during the war. The issue was whether a night shift differential should be paid men working on rotating shifts—the day shift one week, the night shift the next, and so forth. There was neither precedent nor law to supply the answer. We recessed briefly, about ten o'clock. The labor members of the Board went to their office to find out, on phones running to the AFL and CIO, what the labor interest was. The industry members called the NAM and the Chamber of Commerce, to determine the management interest. The three of us called "public" members found ourselves standing beside an open window, looking up at the stars.

In years of "public" membership on tripartite labor boards, sitting between labor and management representatives proceeding from precise instructions, I remember receiving only one piece of advice from those I was supposedly representing. It was a telegram from a member of my family which arrived at a moment of critical doubt in a crucial nationwide strike situation in 1946. It read: "Know you will do whatever you really think is right."

It is important in a democratic government, perhaps even more than in any others, that there be a willingness to make lonely decisions which it is recognized that only a minority would support. Yet something is wrong if this type of decision has to be made very often.

It is not in complaint but in candor that I suggest the difficulties which attend the service of a public interest which is made up in such large measure of a desire for tranquillity. The public wants most of all not to be bothered too much. What is its representative's responsibility in a strike situation when he knows that his constituent is more interested in the strike being settled right now than in its being settled right?

A similar dilemma develops from realization of the public aversion to any kind of "planning" on the part of government officials. It is understandable that there should be an outcry of protest, as there was some time ago, against any attention by the government to the possibility of democracy's defeat in a battle of nations. Clients are always allergic to making wills, and this is right in the case of a nation. It is less comprehensible that there is virtually no interest manifested in this country today in planning for the peace which is the central hope in every human mind and heart.

It is perhaps a contradiction of terms, and inconsistent

with democracy's tenets, to suggest that a public servant look behind public opinion, or pass judgment on the public's frailties. Governments have an alarming tendency to become ends in themselves, and that process starts with some government hired hand deciding to play Caesar instead of Walter Mitty. But this leaves the question of where the correction of this fault is to be made.

My humble but no less firm belief is that democracy's order of things would not last more than a few minutes in history if there were not men in government willing to make unpopular decisions, willing to accept that chill of loneliness that surrounds the responsibility of final decision, affecting other people, based solely on your belief that you are righter than they are.

That cannot be, however, the ultimate answer, for that answer must be in the willingness of people to assume their appointed and essential role in a democracy. Harry Emerson Fosdick said it so well:

> Put yourself into the place of the men in positions of responsibility who at their best are honestly trying to find their way through the jungle to a stable and decent management of the world's affairs. They confront two problems—first, the immensely difficult tasks of political judgment and discrimination, but second, that deeper, haunting question—how far will the people back them up, develop the necessary maturity, make the sacrifices that are required? Are there ethical and spiritual foundations in the people adequate to sustain the kind of world responsibilities we must assume? That question is religious, psychological, and ethical, not political; an affair for which not statecraft but homes, schools, churches, and *multitudes of individuals,* are responsible.

If it is in "a people's judgment that there lies the golden hope of promise," how is that judgment to be arrived at?

I can only describe what seem to me the essential ingredients of that process.

The first of these is the free mind—a mind unshackled by the bonds of self-interest and conformity. Objectivity is not enough. Too much has been said about there always being two sides to every question; there may be only one that is true, and it makes a crucial difference whether truth is put in the first place or the second. Nor is it the point to seek out that position which lies someplace between two others; if one of those positions is right, the middle one is wrong and compromise is intellectual weakness. So there must be, to begin with, a rugged, hard toughening of the mind, to make it not just receptive, but critical of what it receives, searching, open—but only to what can be credited as true.

Yet even such a mental discipline is only a starting point. An open mind is only an engine running well in neutral, and is no good until it is thrown into gear and made to power a forward movement. Robert Frost has reminded that:

> Nature within her inmost self divides
> To trouble men with having to take sides.

So a second element must be knowledge—of the facts of a particular issue, of enough of history that its lessons are not lost, and of all that will illuminate the consequences of decision.

The most serious portent of the future today is not that robots will take over man's work, nor that an exploding population will prove Malthus right, nor that the genes of a future generation will be infected with strontium 90. It is the warning, rather, that the geometrical accumulation of scientific knowledge the world is now experiencing in effect dooms the greater majority of us to live in ignorance of the forces that will control our lives.

There was a great safety factor in man's being subject to what used to be accepted as the laws of nature, laws which most people could by reasonable learning understand. Now the world's scientists have pressed on to a point where these laws are their playthings and where we, charged with the control of those forces, cannot understand them or even communicate meaningfully with those who do. We could, as members of a self-governing society, take a responsible role in shaping a transportation policy involving the movements of horses between towns, or trains and automobiles between distant cities, or even airplanes between continents. Our voice is less effective regarding a policy for the crossing of space between planets by means of a power we cannot comprehend.

This is not, however, the first time man has exposed himself by eating of the fruit of the tree of knowledge. And if it is as an article of faith that we affirm our ability to control as a people what only a few of us know, we will at least narrow the gap between reason's doubt and the assurance of faith by a larger diligence for knowing.

Finally, along with the free mind and knowledge there must be commitment to ultimate values. It is a half-truth to say that government, including self-government, is the art of accomplishing the practicable. That becomes too easily an alibi for conformity, a rationale for mediocrity, a temptation to settle for the status quo. Democracy is a restless, dynamic, animate idea. It is not static, like a beautiful cathedral.

There is no need to prescribe the ultimate values, but danger, rather, in even suggesting what they might be. They include, for me, a commitment to the idea of a future and to the idea of the universality of human opportunity, human dignity and integrity and purpose. But it is enough—and better—that those playing democracy's role guide judgment by commitment to values arrived at as each sees them, in terms of what he knows and believes to be the common good. Our compact with each other as citizens of a free, self-governed society is that we will at all times, under whatever stresses and diversions, lift our sights to where we know they should be and where we know they will have to be for the long pull if we are to realize our common values as individuals and as a nation.

The service of the public interest seems to me, then, the pursuit by free minds, strengthened with knowledge, of ultimate values. If this is a matter of obligation, it is no less one of opportunity. So far as I know yet, life's fullest satisfactions, next to family, come from the privilege of knowing, from the right to think freely, from guiding not by the flashlight of personal avarice but by the stars of humanity's values, from doing what you really think is right, and from sharing a larger responsibility than for your own future.

II

THE POLICIES AND POLITICS OF CHANGE

THE DISCOVERY that change has become the status quo is only a necessary step toward the education of any reasonably intelligent person, and is no matter for pride. What is harder to come by is the development of a legitimate attitude about change, not as a fact but as a good or a bad idea.

There is most to be said for the proposition that change is in itself neither good nor bad, that it has no morals. But if this is true, it is only as a logical abstraction; for there is no heavier chain on the public mind, no firmer brake on the public administrator, than the conviction that a precedent is right until it is proven wrong, a practice innocent until it is proven guilty. This is partly a consequence of laziness and timidity, partly the price of success; for change is a more welcome guest on a bare floor than on wall-to-wall carpeting.

If there is a single common denominator of difference between liberals and conservatives, between labor and management, and between the two political parties in this country, it involves a difference in the attitudes toward change. The general assumptions, on the one hand that change is probably good and on the other that it probably isn't, are perhaps equally intuitive. Yet the effects of these assumptions can determine whether or not advantage is to be taken of the momentum of the times. I confess the prejudice that an inclination to consider change a generally good idea is, in Roger Williams' putting of it, a key to the drawer in which lie other keys.

The Future Is a Good Idea*

The presiding fact in our time is the fact of change, and the common denominator of most of our difficulties is dealing with change honestly and wisely and constructively.

This is not a matter of "adjusting to change." That begs the question, and even implies the wrong answer. It is not a matter of how to be on the defensive against change. It is a matter of how to take the offensive with change, how to make it the implement for man's deliverance instead of the instrument of his destruction.

What is clear when we think of the technology of war is equally real, if less obvious, with respect to the technology of work.

A job used to be something a man expected to have all of his life. If he was a craftsman, he had probably inherited his job from his father and expected to pass it on to his son. The family name often came from the craft—Smith, Mason, Chandler, or Carpenter. A boy growing up in the country walked to school across fields he would probably work the rest of his life. The town boy grew up near a mine or a mill or a plant which was the economic center of the neighborhood's thinking.

This is no longer true. In an era of accelerated change,

* The National Press Club, Washington, D.C., September 25, 1962.

of triumphant technology, of exploding population, where maps change as fast as women's fashions and where continents are now closer together in time than county seats seem to be—in such a time a man's job is the uncertain product of unpredictable but inevitable change.

Within the next thirty days, a half-million people will move to new employers. More than that number will be working on different jobs from those they are working on today. Four hundred thousand will have moved to new labor market areas. A job is no longer something most people can reasonably expect to have or to perform the rest of their lives.

A good many of the recent and current labor disputes reflect the fact that we have not thought out, as a society, the problems which result from the changing concept of work. We are not even doing a very good job of approaching these problems now.

One element of difficulty is the weakness—and the power—of words. Mr. Justice Holmes said once that "The word is the skin of a living thought." A word can also become the shell of a dead idea. Holmes' flattery of words is offset by George Orwell's deeper analysis in his essay "Politics and the English Language." Orwell develops the thought that we have reached the point in politics where we let words do our thinking for us and where the discourse and the dialogue of public affairs become a process of pushing word buttons which evoke certain established reactions, with no "thinking" required of either the speaker or the listener.

Take the words which have dominated the dialogue and the discourse about the problems of labor relations and manpower: "featherbedding," "compulsory arbitration," and "right-to-work laws." These phrases, in our general use of them, corrupt the conversation and prevent the application of understanding to the underlying problem. They have contributed to our seeming to be more concerned with man-hours lost because of "featherbedding" or man-days lost because of strikes than to man-years lost because of unemployment.

The word "featherbedding" has been used to retail the notion that a lot of people don't really want to work, and that this is the significant element in the opposition by some labor unions to technological development. It is truer that this opposition reflects people's wanting very much to work, even to the point that they will resort to the indignity of hanging onto a job which is no longer justified because of their fear of being unable to get another one. The "featherbedding" implication becomes a barrier to rational approach to the very complex problem of technological displacement.

Much of the debate about "compulsory arbitration" results only in stirring up such strong feeling about anything involving "compulsion" that the unquestionable necessity of doing *something* to meet the occasional emergency crisis in collective bargaining is lost sight of.

Regardless of how one feels about "right-to-work" laws, he agrees, if he is honest, that the phrase is a corruption of the English language, because the strongest advocates of those laws have in fact the least intention of recognizing a real "right" to work.

I used to ask my labor law classes a series of questions at the opening session of the course. One question was: "Are you in favor of or opposed to the right-to-work laws?" Two out of three said that they favored such laws. Then a later question was worded this way: "If an employer and a majority of his employees agree with respect to whether all employees should or should not become members of the union, should the government interfere, by law, with that decision?" Two-thirds of the class said they would oppose such a law!

Or take the question of changing the law so as to promote a "thirty-five-hour work week." I disagree with that particular proposal, but it is honorably put. It is not basically a proposal for people to work less, or to make more money. It is essentially a proposal that everyone ought to have an opportunity for a job, and it ought to be considered honestly. Indeed, it seems to me that the only sufficient answer to the proposal for the thirty-five-hour work week is some alternative proposal for producing the jobs which will supply work opportunities to the four million people in this country who want but cannot find them.

We would not be staying up nights in the Labor Department working out "national emergency" disputes if there were a full employment economy in this country. Featherbedding would still be an irritation and an aggravation, but it would not be the problem it is today. The thirty-five-hour work week dispute would disappear. Proposals for compulsory arbitration would be pushed again into the background.

Change requires constructive, honest, straightforward, wise answers to the problems it presents. It is not hard to guide the affairs of a going concern along a course of previous conduct or to represent other people in their contented enjoyment of things as they are or have been all along. The demand today upon the leaders of American labor and industry, upon those of us in public government, and upon the press, is a hard, challenging, tough demand that change be met squarely and that it be made man's servant so that it will not become his master.

If this is a grim prospect for the lazy, the scared, the satisfied, it is an exciting prospect for those who recognize change as the essential quality of growth, who see growth as the distinguishing characteristic of life, and who believe strongly that the future is a good idea.

The Responsibilities of Citizenship*

In a commencement address at Smith College in 1956, poet-philosopher Archibald MacLeish described the decade of the fifties: If you ask, he said, "what the time is like . . . you will get no answerable answer," but only "words which will leave you wondering whether the fifties are really a time at all: whether they are anything more than a time-out, a between times, a limbo . . . not a period in which things are to be done but a period in which things are to be kept from being done, a kind of chronological barbed wire fence to keep history away."

If the fifties were a time out, the intermission is over. If you ask what the sixties are like, I answer that they are a time of turbulent, almost tempestuous change; a time of tearing down barbed wire; a time that will not wait. Most of all they are a time of kinetic, even kaleidoscopic change, which will not blunt, but will demand the "courage of adventurous youth."

Such assessments of the present are advisedly taken with a grain of history. And there are those today who find in the splitting of the atom only another development in that gradual unlocking of nature's forces which began with the

---

* Northern Illinois University Commencement Exercises, De Kalb, Illinois, June 8, 1963.

turning of the first wheel and the lighting of the first fire. There is a certain plausible sophistication in the habit of some to dismiss "automation" as only a new phrase which exaggerates the significance of the current stage of a continuing process which has seen an average annual increase of 3 percent or so in human productivity for the past hundred years.

Such serenity is today a form of sleepwalking. In the past two decades, science has made war obsolete, and has brought into question many of the traditional premises about work. Twenty years ago the maximum price of a human mistake was the destruction of a nation; today it is the extinction of civilization. The change going on in the world today is so unprecedented that it is literally incomprehensible; not change in the sense that it is the thread of all history, but change measurable only in megatons.

There is another, crucial factor in today's situation. There are, roughly, two kinds of change. One is a man's discovery of the forces of nature; the other in his development of his control of those forces, and of himself. Past history is the story of a parallel development of the physical and the social sciences.

There is not that parallel today between the science of things and the science of people. A grimness scars our smile now at James Thurber's warning that "Man is flying too fast for a world that is round. Soon he will catch up with himself, in a great rear-end collision, and Man will never know that what hit Man from behind was Man."

Man is not going to slow up; it would be disastrous if he tried to. There are, to be sure, times in the course of a seemingly insoluble controversy about replacing men with machines when the easy view is that it would have been better if the machines had never been built. But the full employment we seek today depends on pressing as actively as possible the development of new products and more efficient ways of making things. It has been estimated that half of those graduating from college this year will go into occupations which did not exist when they were born. To read of what atomic fallout could do to the human race, or about the grotesque hostages to the development of thalidomide, is to wonder whether it is all worth it. But in the next column is the report that three out of four prescriptions written today are for medicines that were not known twenty-five years ago. If a higher standard of living, leisure, and longer life are important, there can be no argument about the essentiality of technological invention and scientific process.

This leaves, for decision-making, only the other side of the equation: whether we will develop the means of controlling the results of our invention, whether human fulfillment will keep pace with material gain, whether wisdom will catch up with knowledge. "The central need of society," President John Dickey of Dartmouth put it, "is to bring into better balance the utter physical power men now possess as against their moral and political controls of that power."

Why is it that there has developed this disparity in the rate of progress as between science and the control of science, between technology and the technique of human relations?

It is in part that we are educating ourselves as scientists better than as citizens. The physical sciences are in the hands of a few, and the science of human relations is in the hands of many. The scientists have learned their job; the rest of us have not. The scientists' assignments are not easier; they are simply better prepared.

The original and central democratic decision was that government cannot safely, in the long run, be turned over to any few, no matter how wise. That today's problems are harder is no excuse for letting fewer and fewer people decide them; quite the contrary. This means, though, that there must be a larger wisdom in a working majority of all the people. If America's citizen-statesmen do not keep up with what is going on in the common business, that business will not succeed. The continuance of the free society as we know it probably depends on narrowing the present gap between the knowledge of a very few about what can be done with newly harnessed forces of infinite power and the comparative ignorance of these forces on the part of the many who must make the decisions about what should be done with them.

There is no right, in a democracy, to be ignorant. For democracy's principal perquisite is freedom, and freedom is only the converse of responsibility. Freedom is not what the law enforces; it is what people enjoy because of the self-restraint others exercise. It is the unwritten bargain we make with each other; and that bargain must be kept, for the most part, voluntarily. If very much of it is left to the enforcement of the policeman, freedom disappears.

The great advances of science have contributed to that most dangerous illusion in a democracy, that its problems and issues have passed beyond the power of public determination. It cannot be expected that many people can in the future become experts in the fields of science; but they must be able to choose among the experts. If this ability to choose is ever lost, either through indolence or through ignorance, the mortar of democracy will crumble between its building stones.

The scientists and technologists have made war obsolete. They could conceivably do the same thing to work. I do not think they will. But we very much need a working majority of people in this country equipped to cope with both possibilities.

If the need is for fuller knowledge, it is equally for renewed vision. Man cannot live by facts alone. Democracy's need is equally for men and women with a vision of the future that is worthy of a magnificent and growing nation in a rapidly changing world.

In her "Prelude to Independence Address" at Williamsburg, Virginia, in 1963, that remarkable person, Barbara Ward, contrasted America today with America two centuries ago. "The true perspective of 1776," she said, was

> unlimited vision, limited means. . . . The dreams of [the colonists] were palpably ahead of their tools, their ends of their means, their visions of their workaday abilities. The disparity did not daunt them. They simply went ahead to create the first free continental society known to human history.

And today:

> Here, surely, we find ourselves in exactly the opposite position from the men of 1776. Nothing was limited about them except their means. Everything is limited about us except our means. . . . What are our goals? . . . What will be the visions of 1964? Who will dream them? And if free men have no more visions, how soon will the whole great tradition of 1776 perish from the earth?

Dreams? Visions? Yes, or in sterner terms, goals, purposes, and plans—framed, though, not as compromises with circumstance but in the patterns of ideals: plans for full peace that look beyond the stalemate of a cold war; plans for full employment that are based on doing the things that need to be done in this country; plans for full equality of every kind of opportunity for every human being.

Truth and progress are two of the great ideas in democracy's culture. But they will be corrupted if truth becomes only what can be established by the scientific method of proof and progress only a measure of material advance. Truth, in the "provable" sense, is not an end in itself. We have always insisted that there are values which cannot be tested by whether their worth can be proved on paper, in words, statistically. Nor is this any the less true in the face of mortal competition with an alien force which cares nothing for values, or will sacrifice them without qualms to material and military ends.

It would be bitter history if it were later to be recalled that the democracies let themselves become sluggish; that they were stirred from lethargy by Communism's spectacular feats of science; that they were able then to match, and more than match, the Russians' progress in unlocking scientific truth; but that this was accompanied by a lapse in the emphasis on those values which are the essential distinction between democracy and totalitarianism.

In Hawthorne's short story, Ethan Brand, seeking the unpardonable sin, found it in his own breast: "A sin that grew nowhere else! The sin of an intellect that triumphed over the sense of brotherhood with man and reverence for God, and sacrificed everything to its own mighty claims."

This is a time of awesome demands for a wisdom which combines knowledge and vision and values. It is equally a time that offers the fullest promise in history for those who will meet these demands, as individuals and as citizens.

Federalism in Flux*

A familiar point of view depicts the federal government as a monstrous Leviathan, relentlessly expanding as it usurps the resources and prerogatives of state and local governments. The truth is that a quiet revolution has been taking place in American government: in postwar America, public employment has continued to grow, but the overwhelming proportion of this growth has taken place at the state and local level.

Since 1947, almost one-third of the jobs added to the nonagricultural economy have been government jobs, but 88 percent of these have been at the state and local level. In 1962 federal employment was actually 3 percent less than in 1952. Federal workers comprised 4.3 percent of total nonagricultural employment in 1947, and had dropped to 4.2 percent in 1962. For every federal worker added since 1947, nine workers have been added to state or local payrolls. There are present indications of an increase of about 50 percent in state and local government employment by 1975.

Those who specialize in discovering conspiracies may conclude that a plot is afoot to subvert American democracy by increasing the size of state and local governments. Yet what

* Forty-sixth Convention of the International Association of Governmental Labor Officials, Richmond, Virginia, August 21, 1963.

these figures actually reflect, of course, is that the elected state and local government officials of the nation have been responding with vigor, and often with courage, to the changing needs of the people.

Four changes can be clearly discerned, both as they affect the people at large and as they require changes in the activities of state and local government.

First is the vastly increased role of education. In 1962 one out of every two state and local employees was engaged in the educational field. This reflects the central fact of the American economy, that more and more education is required for employment. It is getting to the point where a boy or girl who drops out of high school is practically dropping out of American life. The time is not far off when a large percentage of all workers will need some college training, and will, moreover, need to go back to school in the course of their working lives.

One of the serious inequities of the present federal system is that state and local governments have been required to provide the overwhelming share of the resources needed for education. This is both absurd and dangerous. If there is any one thing holding the nation back from the high level of economic growth which it must achieve, it is that no arrangement has yet worked to channel a sufficient proportion of our national resources into education. When this is done, I predict a surge in the economy more significant than anything brought about by the mass production of automobiles in the 1920's or home appliances in the postwar era. One day soon education is going to be our greatest industry, and it will be a proud day for America.

The second development that has changed the role of

state and local governments might be called urbanism. This has become a nation of city dwellers, required to provide municipal services on an unprecedented level. Thus almost 50 percent of all civil engineers employed in the United States in 1960 were employed either directly in government or in performing government contracts. More than a third of all social scientists such as psychologists and economists were in public service. About one out of every five male technicians in the country works for the government.

A third factor that has brought about a great increase in state and local government services has been the advances in knowledge which have made it possible to do things that were previously impossible. The treatment of mental illness is a singular example. In our lifetimes, almost within the past decade, medical science has so transformed the treatment of mental illness that each year now 1,500,000 patients are treated for conditions that until recently were for practical purposes incurable. Society benefits enormously from this effort, but in the first instance it increases the expenditures of state and local governments.

In February of 1963, President Kennedy sent to the Congress the first comprehensive message on mental illness and mental retardation. He proposed a large-scale program designed particularly to help state and local governments take advantage of medical advances which now make it possible and desirable to treat most mental illness in local community mental health centers. The President proposed that Congress authorize construction grants for 45 to 75 percent of the costs of such local facilities, and thereafter provide up to 75 percent of the initial operating costs. This proposal would reduce considerably the number of persons in public employment, or at least those working for the federal or state governments. Until very recently, patients in our mental hospitals have usually been wards of the state, and their physicians and nurses state employees. The President's proposal is for federal assistance that will help return treatment of mental illness to the community, and, often as not, put it out of government channels entirely, into the channels of local, voluntary hospitals.

A fourth condition that has brought about an increase in state and local government has been the emergence of what has come to be called structural unemployment. Until recently in the nation, we have been accustomed to thinking of economic conditions essentially in national terms. Similarly, government activity in economic matters has been largely at the national level, through the adoption of federal fiscal policies, tariff policies, and the wide range of recovery measures that emerged under the New Deal. Of late, it has become clear that a considerable amount of economic difficulty is not directly related to general economic movements, and that some groups and areas can be in great difficulty even though the nation as a whole is doing quite well.

This development has clearly called for greater state and local efforts to deal with specific state and local conditions. Hence the remarkable and healthy growth of economic development agencies throughout the nation. The Area Redevelopment Act and the Manpower Development and Training Act are major contributions to efforts of state and local governments to deal with the problems of structural unemployment, and, of course, both programs provide for extensive federal-state local cooperation.

All this adds up to many things, but it comes first of all in almost every state to a more or less continual fiscal strain. In the decade from 1953 to 1962 state expenditures more than doubled, from $16.9 billion to $36.4 billion. From 1950 to 1962 state debt increased by more than 400 percent, rising from about $5.5 billion to $22 billion.

There is no turning back for state and local government. There is no question but that this rate of increase will continue. The only real question before the nation is whether we will adopt those measures necessary to reach and maintain a high level of economic growth that will produce from the present revenue structures of state and local governments sufficient income to provide the services that are needed.

This is first of all a question of expanding job opportunities. But economic growth alone will not do the whole job. Whatever the level of the gross national product, there will remain workers without jobs, and areas with declining prosperity, unless there are special efforts to meet the problems of structural unemployment caused by the ever-accelerating changes in technology.

One of the main instruments of an active national labor market policy to deal with such problems is an effective public employment service, administered on a continued state-federal partnership basis. Arthur Goldberg put it well when he was Secretary of Labor: "A modernized Employment Service must assume that the action front will remain—as it is now—within the local offices—operated by the States, but also as an integral part of a national system of public employment offices." It is equally clear that at a time of basic change in the characteristics of unemployment in the economy the terms of this partnership warrant close attention to insure their effectiveness in meeting new demands.

There is an unfortunate rigidity regarding this federal-state relation. Repeatedly—in the consideration, for example, of any new administrative proposal—reactions are immediately polarized in terms of whether the new suggestion would affect, even by a degree, the previous balance of federal and state authority. Battle lines are drawn before the issues are. The question of whether the idea is good or bad, whether it would mean more or less unemployment, gets deferred, and sometimes lost.

The dialogue in this area has become infected with false arguments. It is a false argument that because the federal government collects and disburses the tax monies which support the employment and unemployment programs it is entitled to make all the decisions or do the whole job. It is a half-truth that state agencies gain a superior wisdom from their closer proximity to local problems, unless the debilitating effects of larger exposure to distinctive local pressures are also recognized. And the whole states' rights argument is false when it is used not to gain local responsibility but rather as a tactic to oppose anything being done at all.

In a surprising number of cases it turns out that those who show up in Washington to oppose new federal action on the ground that it invades states' rights take evening planes for the state capitals to argue there the next morning that the states are too impoverished to take any such action themselves. And behind many a pious argument against some proposed shift in the balance of state and federal responsibility is a much homelier concern about preserving a handful of sinecures.

It will help greatly to agree that the question is going to be, not who is right, but what is right. The problems at hand should be approached with as great a readiness to concede the dangers of centralized control as to assert its potential efficiency, and with as large a willingness to recognize state responsibilities as state rights.

There are difficulties enough ahead, and unequaled opportunities. The federal system of government, now almost two centuries old, has rarely exhibited such vigor as it has these past few years with the unparalleled growth in the activities of state and local governments. As never before, we can look to a period when states and localities can genuinely become a source of new ideas, of experiment and of innovation. It is for us, as President Kennedy put it, "to weave from all these tangled threads a fabric of law and progress . . . joining together, seeking as our forefathers sought, to find freedom in diversity and unity in strength."

The Politics of Change*

The story of the railroad case that started in 1959 and continued unsettled for four and a half years is the story of men, the negotiators in that case, who fell back gradually onto the assumption that their problem was too big for them to settle, and that someone else would have to settle it for them. This is the most dangerous assumption the people of a free society can make.

That assumption was dispelled by President Johnson's simple but firm insistence that the price of freedom is the exercise of private responsibility. It was at the end of one night's long bargaining session that he said quietly, "Before you give up, and decide that the system of free decision we operate under won't work, look around the world and be clear about what other system you are going to choose instead."

The settlement reaffirms the power and effectiveness of free, private decision-making, with government acting only as a catalyst of free people's basic sense of shared responsibility.

So will the larger problems we face be settled.

There is a proper function of law: to crystallize now the national consensus that racial discrimination is intolerable,

* National Democratic Women's Conference, Washington, D.C., May 1, 1964.

that the denial of adequate hospital care is an indecent penalty on old age, that poverty is an infection that weakens and demeans a proud and prosperous people, that ignorance and lack of education must and can be removed from the American bloodstream. The immediate task at hand is to pass the Civil Rights Bill, the Medicare Bill, and the Economic Opportunities Act.

But the larger task is to mobilize the power for good that lies in people's essential willingness and desire to assume responsibility for something more than their own personal condition. The force which will shape the future is the force which was reflected in young America's response to the Peace Corps program. That force was manifest in the nation's response to John F. Kennedy's call upon his countrymen to consider what they could do for their country, and is embodied, today, in the still deep, burning desire to discover a way to memorialize a spirit no bullet could reach or destroy. That force motivates the response now to President Lyndon B. Johnson's declaration of an unconditional war on poverty.

It is this force which is today being summoned to produce answers to the problems of discrimination and disadvantage, of automation, and of animosity between nations when there is none between the people of those nations.

If there is a political issue here, it does not lie in any differences between the magnanimity or the humanity of people of different political persuasion. It lies rather in differences in attitudes toward change and toward the need to activate what is within us if we are to meet the demands of change. President Johnson has said, "Change is inevitable. The question is whether it will be orderly and constructive or disorderly and destructive."

The future's facts are that by 1975: there will be ten million more families than there are today, and eight million more students in college—twice the present number; the Gross National Product will be almost a trillion dollars a year; there will be 93 million people in the work force; per capita income will be 50 percent greater than it was in 1960. We must know these facts for what they require and for what they offer.

Time to talk politics? Yes. It is always time to talk politics: the politics of belief in the promise of change, that the national purpose is the human purpose, that progress is measured only in the fullness of people's lives, and that the test is not the success of some but the opportunity which is given to all. The basic political issue is between those who are satisfied with what is good and those who insist on what is better.

For fifty years the Democratic Party has been the instrument of change in America. The New Freedom, the New Deal, the Fair Deal, the New America, the New Frontier, the Great Society—these are not just campaign slogans; they are the heart beat of a party and a people standing always as at the dawn, aware of what the day offers, and ready to seize its fullest promise.

III

FREE AND CONSTRUCTIVE COLLECTIVE BARGAINING

RECENT DEVELOPMENTS in collective bargaining suggest that a new note of common responsibility for the common good is being added to our economic theme. It equates capitalism with economic democracy, and recognizes that the essential characteristic of democracy is voluntary respect for someone else's interests. This is not, however, the product of a rising morality of attitudes, but is an application, rather, of the iron law of necessity.

The central question about collective bargaining is whether or not this new element of broader responsibility will suffice to allow the system to function under the strains imposed by technological change, or whether such bargaining will be supplemented—and I think greatly weakened—by the adoption of some form of "compulsory arbitration."

I think, in this connection, of the receipt in the Department of Labor, during the thirty-day strike by the Telegraphers against the Chicago & Northwestern Railroad in 1962, of some 3,500 telegrams. They came largely from the owners of business and commercial enterprises which were being hurt by the strike. Almost all of these wires urged and demanded that the government move into that case on whatever basis was necessary to stop the strike. Yet almost all of those who took this position would be opposed, in general, to "more government."

The public's view of collective bargaining is affected largely by the single fact of whether it results in peaceful settlements or in strikes; and there is little expressed or felt concern about whether the terms of settlement which are arrived at comport with the general welfare or are at variance with it. In general, the public dislikes the idea of collective bargaining, but tolerates it because of the realization that the only alternative would be a debilitating degree of governmental decision-making.

The resort by Congress to a form of compulsory arbitration in the 1963 railroad case reduced rather than increased the likelihood of similar action in the future. It became clear in that experience how widespread the feeling is that governmental "interference" with collective bargaining must be avoided at almost any cost. President Johnson's quiet admonition to the parties, at a later stage in that case, to consider "what other systems you are going to choose instead," says it all pretty well.

New Developments in Collective Bargaining*

The play *The Miracle Worker* is the story of how a teacher, Annie Sullivan, broke through the barriers of blindness and deafness behind which an otherwise gifted five-year-old child had withdrawn to a state of bitterness and virtual bestiality. By almost unbelievable patience and understanding, but with equal and sometimes grim discipline and determination, Annie Sullivan eventually worked the miracle which the world later came to know as Helen Keller.

Twenty-five years ago there were in the relationship between American labor and American management elements of intransigence and hatred comparable in their way to those which threatened to destroy the infinite potential of the frustrated child Annie Sullivan first came to. That was the period of the sit-down strike and the "Mohawk Valley formula," the time when the now respected John L. Lewis was a personal devil in the minds of management and pickets faced Pinkertons outside locked gates patrolled by armed guards.

During these twenty-five years, a group of perhaps two hundred men have devoted their professional lives to trying

* Wharton School of Finance and Commerce, Philadelphia, Pennsylvania, May 26, 1961; Labor-Management Day Luncheon, International Trade Fair, Chicago, Illinois, August 3, 1961.

to contribute to this relationship, as arbitrators, mediators, "neutrals," what Annie Sullivan gave Helen Keller: the key to her own power. The success of this effort has been due in large measure to a man who has served as teacher of many of those two hundred, as a private arbitrator himself, as public official, as artisan and architect of American labor-management relations. I have waited a long time for an opportunity to say what is much more than a personal "thank you" to this Miracle Worker—George W. Taylor.

There is a broader purpose in this salutation. These twenty-five years have brought collective bargaining a long way forward. The relationship now is one in which labor and management have developed a self-sufficiency for concord and for cooperation. The role for the third party is, arguably, diminished. And yet if there is a single dominant emphasis in the discussion of collective bargaining today, it is about the necessity of its taking a still larger account of the "public interest." The need for "miracle workers" is less than before; but it is being insisted that in one form or another the public be recognized, if not at the bargaining table itself, at least in the decisions that are made there.

The prospects of hanging, Dr. Johnson observed, tend to concentrate one's thoughts greatly. Developments of this decade are producing a new awareness of the elements of the common interest, and a quickening to anything that may appear to threaten that interest. A cold war continues. Rising imports bring a new realization of increasing world competition. Mounting juvenile delinquency rates bring home, as unemployment statistics could not, the fact that increased millions of younger workers are hitting the job market, finding too few jobs, and turning to making trouble. A technological breakthrough has been given a new name—automation—and the fear is developing that machines will replace men and women in industry and commerce.

Most of these developments are not immediately thought of as matters of labor-management relations. Yet it is obvious that these scientific, demographic, political, and economic earthquakes are bound to affect greatly, perhaps basically, not only wages and hours and seniority rights and employment generally, but also the procedures and the motive forces of collective bargaining. What is perhaps less clear is that these developments raise new questions about the relationship of the "public" and the "private" functions and responsibilities so far as the employment relationship is concerned. Any suggestion that such developments fall entirely outside the competence of collective bargaining would have far-reaching implications so far as the future of this process is concerned.

If company representatives say, at the bargaining table, "We won't discuss what happens to the people we have to lay off when we bring in new equipment; we're in business to make a profit, not to run a charity ward," they in effect leave it to the government to take over a responsibility, the discharge of which they will then later condemn, probably as "socialism."

If union representatives meet that same problem by insisting that permanent sinecures be arranged for men who are no longer actually needed in the plant, they weaken collective bargaining by using it to produce a wrong answer, which will not stand up, for an economy that must achieve its full growth cannot afford a manpower waste.

If a company and a union agree on a wage increase which

will require a price increase making the product noncompetitive as against foreign goods, and then put "Buy American" stickers on their automobiles and go to Washington to demand higher tariffs or import quotas, they use collective bargaining to sap the strength of the national economy.

These are the key problems in labor relations today. Unless collective bargaining has answers to offer, it will be relegated in the future to matters of housekeeping in the plant: administering procedures for handling discharge cases, establishing safety programs, devising senority systems that don't cover the crucial cases, and dividing up pies the size of which is determined someplace else. The continuation of private collective bargaining as the important force in the future it has been in the past depends on the decision of the bargainers to exercise responsibility for the concerns that affect the whole economy.

These "public" concerns are not easily defined. They include the achievement of an equitable sharing of the costs and the fruits of production or service, finding the meaning of "equitable" more in experience than in logic. They include the maintenance of economic stability and the avoidance of spiraling inflation. The "public interest" includes, perhaps most significantly today, the achievement of the nation's full capacity for economic growth.

Yet the question remains of how, even whether, collective bargaining can, at its best, provide adequate response to such problems as technological displacement, or the reconciliation of high standards of living and free trade as coordinate national objectives.

There is increasing evidence of significant efforts to take account of the broad and basic realities of this developing situation. Some of these are reflected in the normal processes of bargaining, by the inclusion, as just one example, of such things as severance pay provisions. But what is even more noteworthy is the emergence of basically new patterns of collective bargaining, or, more broadly, of labor-management relationships.

In the construction industry, for example, there is not only the National Joint Board for the Settlement of Jurisdictional Disputes, but also the National Disputes Adjustment Plan between the Building Trades and National Construction Association, and the Joint Appeals Board established by the Building Trades and the Associated General Contractors.

Until the early 1950's the coal fields were battlegrounds of belligerence bordering so close to apparent anarchy that President Truman considered seriously drafting miners into the army. Today the bituminous coal operators, the United Mine Workers, the utilities which are the principal users of coal, as well as the railroads which carry it, are members of the National Coal Policy Conference, whose jurisdiction, as its most famous architect describes it, is "anything we can agree on." There hasn't been a major coal strike since 1950.

The National Coat and Suit Industry Recovery Board is another example of much the same thing. By broadening out the area of recognized mutual interests of the industry and the union, a basis has been found for moving away from trial by combat and toward an at least more peaceful form of decision-making.

Another type of cooperation is reflected in the establishment of funds to finance additional employment opportunities, retraining or relocation for employees displaced by technological change. A Music Performance Trust has been established by the Musicians and the recording companies after a lengthy strike caused by the increasing use of "canned" music. Financed by contributions from the record companies on their sales, this fund has contributed to the enjoyment of millions of Americans by sponsoring free concerts by "live" musicians. Armour & Company and the Meat Cutters and Packinghouse Workers have entered into an agreement intended to cushion whatever unemployment may arise through the introduction of automation in meat packing by financing a study of displacement problems and by sponsoring retraining programs. The Pacific Maritime Association and the West Coast Longshoremen's agreement guarantees wages in return for removal of work restrictions. A contract between the International Brotherhood of Electrical Workers and a West Coast manufacturer of automated broadcasting equipment establishes a fund for retraining the employees of purchasers of such equipment who are displaced by it.

It does not diminish the significance of these developments to suggest that they probably reflect less the emergence of an era of labor-management goodwill than they do the sentiment that drew the Butcher and the Beaver together in Lewis Carroll's *Hunting of the Snark*:

> The valley grew narrow and narrower still
> And the evening grew darker and colder
> 'Til (merely from nervousness, not from goodwill)
> They marched along shoulder to shoulder.

Or, in Mr. Justice Holmes' phrase, it may be said that the collective bargaining procedure is responding to "the felt necessities of the times."

There is increasing evidence, too, that in the meeting of

these new demands there will probably develop new forms of cooperative action between labor and management on the one hand and "government" on the other.

Any such development will be critically appraised, and properly so. Although we speak affectionately of the idea of government of and by and for the people, we also attribute to it a separate, almost anthropomorphic personality. We fight "its" taxes, condemn its policies as though we had nothing to do with making them, and count its agents more as our antagonists than our employees—a view some of them occasionally seem to share. We find it convenient, furthermore, to ignore the pluralistic facts of life and to think of political decision-making and economic decision-making as functions much more separate from each other than we know they actually are.

Yet here again necessity is mothering at least a changing attitude, a type of invention.

There is, for example, the procedure which has been established for the handling of labor disputes at the missile and space sites.

Reports of excessive work interruption and petty profiteering at these sites have aroused national indignation. The temptation to compromise democratic principles and the ideas of self-government when such things happen on the front lines of the cold war is always strong. There have been insistent demands that the government move in on the missile site situation on a strong-arm basis. Instead, President Kennedy has set up, at the suggestion of Secretary of Labor Arthur Goldberg, a Missile Sites Labor Commission made up of government officials, public representatives, and leaders of American labor and management. The private statesmen have pledged complete cooperation in this new procedure, including pledges against strikes or lockouts. Strong reliance is placed, in the Executive Order establishing the Commission, on private and voluntary dispute settlement procedures at the missile sites, with the authority of the government being put behind these procedures. The Commission will provide forums for settling peaceably and rationally those labor disputes and problems which would otherwise result in strikes or other resorts to economic force.

A different kind of cooperative private-public distribution of functions is emerging in connection with the matter of worker displacement resulting from automation. After thorough study of this situation, the committee established by Armour and the Packinghouse Workers reached the conclusion that: "Only through a coordinated approach in which public policy and private action mutually reinforce one another can the employment problems of technological change be met. Collective bargaining by itself cannot fully solve these problems."

It is clear that a substantial part of the retraining job will fall, at least for the time being, upon the government. The Manpower Development and Training Act is a major effort to discharge this responsibility. But this program, like the related Employment Service program, will be effective only as there can be full cooperation between private industry and the government agencies which are involved. In Sweden there has developed a virtually uniform practice of employers advising the Labor Market Board whenever they face the prospect of displacing any significant number of employees, so that retraining and reassignment procedures can immediately be instituted; which is at least part of the reason why the unemployment rate in Sweden is down to less than 2 percent.

There is the parallel development of increasing reliance, in those matters where the initiative is with the government, on advisory or decision-making boards which bring to the government's benefit the advantage of private counsel and close working with the parties. The most significant development in this area is the creation of the President's Advisory Committee on Labor-Management Policy. This Committee, which includes fourteen leaders of American management and American labor, meets at the White House regularly with seven representatives of the public, including the Secretary of Labor and the Secretary of Commerce, to develop that consensus which will help the President discharge his responsibilities in the areas of labor-management relations, technological development, and our competitive position in world trade.

This, then, seems the likely future course of collective bargaining if it is to preserve its meaningfulness: that it will take larger account of the responsibilities which the new forces loose in the world have created; that its procedures will continue to develop along new lines which make it a more reasoned sort of process; and that there will be a converging and a coordination of public and private decision-making in the whole area of labor relations. There will be, in short, more reliance in collective bargaining on the principles of government, more use in government of the resources and procedures of collective bargaining, and more coordination of the two processes.

Constructive Bargaining*

A recent letter from one of the nation's most respected citizens, Bernard M. Baruch, expresses a concern which is today much in people's minds. Referring to what he identifies—with the gentility of understatement—as a recent "succession of labor-management quarrels," Mr. Baruch observes that

> while the rights and interests of labor and of business must be respected, the rights and interests of the public deserve at least equal consideration. . . . Both labor and business have sufficient power . . . to pursue courses which too often are at variance with the public interest. Too many of the struggles between these two are not only waged at the public's expense but are settled at it.

Recalling his recommendation after World War I that there be established a High Court of Commerce, which would "have jurisdiction over labor-management issues which the parties themselves could not resolve," Mr. Baruch concluded: "I think such a body—a Court of Labor-Management Relations—is even more necessary today."

This proposal must be set entirely aside from that body of current reaction to what is typically identified—in a phrase which signals its predilection and prejudice—as "the labor problem." That reaction fixes on the image of one

* National Academy of Arbitrators, Chicago, Illinois, February 1, 1963.

notorious union official, despite the evidence from three and a half years now of active administration of the Labor-Management Reporting and Disclosure Act of 1959 that a high level of integrity and democracy obtains in organized labor as a whole. That general reaction also typically expresses a fear of excessive labor pressures in terms of alarm about inflation, despite the fact that this is the fourth year now of almost unprecedented price stability and that the rate of advance in wages has been steadily diminishing. Or there is professed outrage about labor's broad combinations, ignoring the implications of the illustrative fact of New York City's being virtually without newspapers when five publications are shut down by the publishers because four others were struck by the printers.

Even the concern about economy-crippling strikes must be set in context. Lost time and production from strikes has, during the past three years, represented a smaller percentage (about one-seventh of one percent) of total man-hours worked than during any other years since the end of the last war. It is an illuminating, if only partially valid, comparison, that more potential man-hours of production were lost in 1962 as the result of involuntary unemployment than had been lost from all strikes in the previous thirty-five years. The public reacts more vehemently to a kick in the shins than to an attack of economic arthritis.

A separately identifiable issue was nevertheless precipitated when the steel industry, basic to the entire economy, was shut down for 116 days in 1959. That same issue arose again when seven airlines were closed down suddenly, if only briefly, in 1961; when all shipping was stopped on the East Coast for eighteen days that same year; when all West Coast ports were closed three times during 1961 and 1962; when most building construction was stopped for substantial periods during 1962 in New York City, Northern California, and the Pacific Northwest; and when a railroad in the Midwest did not run for thirty days in the fall of 1962. This issue emerged even more clearly in early 1963, with the thirty-eight-day shutdown of all East Coast and Gulf ports because of the longshoremen's strike, two-month newspaper blackouts in two major cities, and the putting of production of the Polaris and Minute Man missiles under the last-ditch protection of eighty-day injunctions.

There have been comparable periods of crisis before—right after World War I, for example; during the sit-down strikes of the late thirties; and with the coincidence of coal, railroad, and steel strikes in the late forties. Nevertheless, those most sensitive to the dynamics of labor-management relations and to the relevance in this area of broader economic and political developments recognize significantly new elements in this situation.

One such element is that most of these recent controversies have involved basic issues of manpower utilization and job security. Technological developments have placed severe new strains on collective bargaining. It is one thing to bargain about terms and conditions of employment, and quite another to bargain about the terms of unemployment, about the conditions on which men are to yield their jobs to machines.

A second element in the present situation is that the public tolerance for strikes is diminishing rapidly. This is partly a matter of economics. With the increasing specialization of functions in the economy, and with the increasing interdependence of its units, more nonparticipants are hurt worse and faster by a shutdown than used to be the case. We have always insisted that competition—which includes competition between employers and employees—is worth what it costs the rest of us; but the cost has been going up. It is more frequently true now than it used to be that a shutdown will hurt the public badly before it hurts one or the other party to it enough that someone has to cry "uncle."

Strike benefit programs for striking employees and strike insurance programs for employers are intensifying this factor. It was a significant fact in the New York newspaper case that during most of its first month the printers were receiving up to ninety dollars a week in strike benefits and the publishers were sharing in a substantial strike insurance program.

This is also a matter of a changing national psychology. Strikes, regardless of who is responsible for them, are waste; and it is part of the cold war psychology that the nation's tolerance for waste is lowered.

It is logical to conclude, even after applying the necessary discount rate to trials and tribulations of the moment, that we stand today at what history will probably mark as a fairly clear fork in the development of labor-management relations in this country. Neither the traditional collective bargaining procedures nor the present labor dispute laws are working to the public's satisfaction, at least so far as major labor controversies are concerned. It does not matter how much the hurt has been real, or has been exaggerated. A decision has been made, and that decision is that if collective bargaining can't produce peaceable settlements of these controversies, the public will.

The present period seems to be a holding period, during

which traditional collective bargaining is being given, in the lawyer's phrase, its last clear chance. This is the real significance of the record of the federal government's unusual participation recently in a number of the major disputes which have developed. This is a record with which I profess some familiarity—the familiarity, roughly, an egg has with an egg beater. It is a record, essentially, of improvisation.

Settlement of the last round of contract disputes in the airline industry took over two years, and involved the President of the United States, the Secretary of Labor, the Under Secretary of Labor, the National Mediation Board, a Special Presidential Commission, nine Presidential Emergency Boards, and three Boards of Arbitration—a total of thirty-nine public representatives. That this meant part-time employment to twenty-four members of the National Academy of Arbitrators will not, I think, commend it to many of the membership as a wholly satisfactory, or efficient, government procedure.

In the recent longshore case, the public participants, during its twelve-month course, were the President, the Secretary of Labor, an Assistant Secretary of Labor, the Director of the Federal Mediation and Conciliation Service, his Deputy, fifteen FMCS mediators, a Taft-Hartley Board of Inquiry, the Attorney General, the Federal District Court, the mayors of numerous port cities, a Special Presidential Board which was appointed but never convened, and another special board under the chairmanship of a U.S. Senator.

There were times, in the course of these marathons of maneuver, when the only promise for parties and public participants alike seemed to be the reminder, from "The Garden of Proserpine," of Swinburne's consoling thought:

We thank with brief thanksgiving
Whatever gods may be . . .
That even the weariest river
Winds somewhere safe to sea.

Such a program of improvisation clearly offers too little for the long-run future. As each new device or expedient is used, its utility diminishes; what may work in one case because it is spectacular loses its effectiveness when it becomes commonplace. Immunities are built up to procedures and pressures which depend in large measure on the evanescent virtue of novelty. These measures have been resorted to both because of a public demand of much greater intensity than can be generally realized, and to prevent collective bargaining from committing suicide.

There has been a good deal of discussion of this experience in terms of the enervating influence upon collective bargaining, and upon more traditional forms of legislatively prescribed procedures, of any special form of intervention. This question is properly raised. So is the question of whether, had these steps not been taken, collective bargaining would by this time have been replaced, to a significant extent, by some form of statutory decision-making.

Neither question can ever be definitively answered. It is clear that in most of these cases collective bargaining, as well as the issue in the particular controversy, was on trial. The public interest involved was both the public interest in avoiding or ending a serious interruption of the economy and the public interest—as most of us here would see it—in preserving collective bargaining as an essentially free, private process. Too many of those closest to collective bargaining today—labor, management, and public representatives alike

—seriously underestimate the strength of the public feeling about national emergency strikes, and the brinkmanship we have been playing in this field.

What, then, of the future?

There appear to be two possibilities.

One is that another major crisis will develop, and that no sufficiently new and effective improvisation on the theme of Taft-Hartley can be devised. In that event, the very real likelihood is that there will be developments along the line of the Baruch proposal. He has set out his suggestion in some detail:

> What is needed is a Court of Labor-Management Relations which would have jurisdiction to settle strikes when, in the President's judgment, the national interest is jeopardized by their continuation and after the collective bargaining processes and the provisions of the Taft-Hartley Act have been exhausted. This Court, composed of representatives from Labor, Business and the Public, should have the power after hearing evidence from the contesting parties to hand down decisions binding upon both.

I think such a development would be exceedingly unfortunate. Arbitration is thought of, and recommended, as a substitute for strikes. It would become, if required by statute, a substitute for bargaining.

Experience, particularly the War Labor Board experience during the forties, confirms that a statutory requirement that labor disputes be submitted to arbitration has a narcotic effect on private bargainers, that they turn to it as an easy and habit-forming release from the obligation of hard, responsible bargaining. The difficulty is that in virtually every dispute one bargainer or the other feels that his chances are better, or that he can evade responsibility for a hard decision, if he lets the issue go to arbitration. No effective way has yet been devised or suggested of limiting the availability of such procedures to cases in which "the collective bargaining processes . . . have been exhausted." The record is that if arbitration is assured, the collective bargaining processes are never really used at all.

It is easy to agree that the public interest will be most fully served in a particular case by prohibiting a strike and requiring the parties to submit their dispute to a third party. There is also the public interest in leaving as many decisions as possible to private processes.

But free collective bargaining can no longer depend on the defense that compulsory arbitration is evil. Nor does its protection lie in endless new administrative resourcefulness and maneuver. The preservation of free collective bargaining depends on two necessary developments.

One of these has to do with the health of the economy as a whole. It is questionable whether serious and difficult issues arising from the displacement, or threatened displacement, of men by machines or by new work methods can be satisfactorily dealt with in major industries by free collective bargaining unless the economy is developing at a rate which will give displaced employees reasonable assurance of an opportunity to find other jobs. If there is not that assurance, they will probably deny their bargaining representatives the authority to negotiate for their discard. The future of free collective bargaining is probably linked closely to the future employment rate.

Beyond this, the future of collective bargaining, free of the weakening effects of statutory arbitration procedures, depends upon the development of private procedures which will permit and virtually assure the settlement of major disputes in critical industries without crippling shutdowns. There is significant evidence that this development is taking place today in a highly meaningful degree and at a rapidly accelerating pace.

It is common to most of the recent emergency dispute cases that the settlements reached have included significant arrangements for meeting, and hopefully avoiding, another crisis. This was true of the 1959-60 steel settlement, of the 1962 settlement in the airlines cases, and of the 1963 settlement in the longshore case.

Active discussion is presently going on among responsible men on both sides of the bargaining tables in most major industries, looking for a better way to meet their problems. What is developing is much more than collective bargaining in the old sense of the term. It is constructive bargaining, or, perhaps even better, creative bargaining.

Although these programs vary in detail, most of them include three elements:

First, arrangements are being worked out to deal during the contract period with those problems, such as adjustment to automation, which are so involved that they cannot be dealt with during the count-down period at the end of the contract. This will provide the forums, and the time, to develop the new ideas which are so badly needed to meet the problems of a work force which is today in flux—ideas which will be the counterpart of such innovations, for example, as the cost-of-living and productivity increase which General Motors and the Automobile Workers developed a decade ago.

Second, most of these programs involve the use in one form or another of neutral or third parties, as advisers or consultants or fact-finders. The participation in these private negotiations of third persons who are independent in the full sense of the term offers a considerable measure of protection of the public interest, and more than the actually effective public interest which in most cases is only in wanting a settlement to be reached peacefully.

The third element in most of these programs is one form or another of special arrangement for approaching as constructively as possible the crucial bargaining which will move the parties from one contract period to the next. Some of these arrangements provide for arbitration—voluntary arbitration, adjusted to the particular circumstances. Others meet the pressing need for more orderly and responsible arrangements between the several employer units which are involved, or within the union group. Part of the problem has been in moving into "unity" bargaining of one kind or another without working out the stresses and strains within one group or the other, or both.

In addition to these significant indications of private interest in new and healthier forms of bargaining, there are encouraging signs of the responsive adjustment of government programs to facilitate this development. Both the Federal Mediation and Conciliation Service and the National Mediation Board are working with the parties in many instances now long before the contract expiration crisis arises. We are exploring in the Department of Labor possible ways of applying more directly to particular industry and company situations what has previously been for the most part general research. Perhaps there should be developed an extension service in this area, supplying assistance comparable to that which the Department of Agriculture gives to farmers.

Charged by agreement of the longshoring companies and the International Longshoremen's Association with making a study of their manpower utilization and job security problems, to facilitate their working these problems out before the next contract showdown, we realize that if this had been done in 1960, the longshore debacle of 1962-63 might have been avoided.

Perhaps it should probably be considered whether government procurement contracts should require that suppliers take maximum steps to assure against interruptions of production, just as the Equal Employment Opportunities program establishes norms in these procurement contracts for nondiscriminatory hiring practices.

It would be a mistake to suggest that whatever this is that can be called constructive or creative bargaining is something clearly identifiable. The suggestion may derive as much from the realization of new and critical need as from the recognition of actual experience. It may well be an entirely different formulation or suggestion that will eventually meet this need. The established institution of free collective bargaining faces a challenge which arises in significant part from the advances of science, the new discoveries of the technologists.

Why is it that there is such an obvious, in some ways ominous, predominance today of scientific over institutional invention? It is not, surely, that the physical scientist is wiser than his political counterpart. Is he freer, less afraid to question, to probe, to propound ideas that are different? Is it that the centuries have reversed the roles since that time when scientists were condemned as heretics for their innovations while politicians—in the higher sense—were saluted for working out democracy's beginnings? May this be democracy's ultimate testing against an alien society where the dictator's decree has no constraint upon it?

Ambassador Adlai Stevenson has said, "We have learned that modern technology can strengthen the despot's hand and the dictator's grasp—and for that reason, if no other, we know that democracy is more necessary now than it ever was. But democracy is not self-executing. We have to make it work." Collective bargaining is industrial democracy. We have to make it work.

The Press and Labor Relations*

The 1963 breakdowns of collective bargaining on the New York and Cleveland newspapers have resulted in new insistence that the functions of the press in the society and economy require finding better ways than strikes and lockouts to settle labor-management disputes in the fourth estate.

To the extent that these suggestions rely upon the constitutional guarantee of freedom of the press, they warrant reminder that this particular freedom involves more a right of the public than of any private person or interest. Arthur Hays Sulzberger said of the constitutional recognition of the importance of the press that it "is the statement of an essential liberty of a free people and not a grant of immunity extended to a particular trade or profession. . . . The responsibilities that the franchise entails are greater than the privileges it bestows."

What is involved is the public's right to know—not just to look at something, from comic strips to market quotations, but to know those important facts and that essential truth without which democracy cannot function properly. It is only to the extent that a particular newspaper supplies these commodities of critical fact and truth that the shutdown of that

* American Society of Newspaper Editors, Washington, D.C., April 19, 1963.

paper is any different from the shutdown of any other plant or operation.

Perhaps it confuses two issues to suggest that if the test were to be the handling by the press of matters relating to labor-management relations, it would be difficult to identify a discharge of responsibility warranting special measures to protect against the interruption of that function. For it is distressingly true in the labor relations area that good news, reversing the adage, is considered no news. A strike gets extended coverage. The peaceful signing of a new collective bargaining agreement, even in a major industry, is at best a one-day story, usually on an inside page. When collective bargaining works, as it does in the great majority of cases, that isn't news. When, occasionally, it doesn't, that is news —bad news which affects significantly the public's judgment about one of democracy's essential procedures.

It is no sufficient explanation that people won't buy papers to read about peace, either among nations or between companies and unions. If there is a case for special procedures to prevent, or reduce the possibilities of, interruption of newspaper publication by labor disputes, it necessarily depends on the exercise by the press of some higher degree of public responsibility than what is involved in the indulgence of reader appetites which will maximize the number of newspapers that can be sold. If there is no such higher standard of press responsibility, then there is no more reason for such special procedures here than there is for procedures to assure uninterrupted satisfaction of consumer desires for cigarettes or cosmetics.

There is, of course, a higher standard. It lies in the disciplined determination of what presentation of the news will give the American public the fullest, most objective basis for making up its mind about the things that count. It is respect for this standard of responsibility on the part of the press that warrants the conclusion that protracted interruptions of the discharge of this responsibility cannot properly or safely be tolerated by a society being put today to new tests of its central belief that all the people are more reliable decision-makers than just a few, or one or two.

There have been proposals that it be required, by law, that any irreconcilable labor dispute in a newspaper case be submitted to arbitration. Some add the sugar coating of a suggestion that the submission be to "labor courts." Such a procedure would end strikes and lockouts in the newspaper industry. It would also end collective bargaining in this industry, and would probably spread to other industries as well. It would be bitterest irony if freedom of the press were to become the standard under which the freedom of collective bargaining was destroyed. What is called for instead is a fuller exercise, in specific, meaningful form, of private responsibility.

There is a clear distinction to be made between arbitration required by law and arbitration agreed upon voluntarily by the parties. There is today a procedure for arbitration in the Pressmen's contract with the American Newspaper Publishers' Association. There were twenty years of experience with an even broader arbitration procedure involving the Printers and the Association. The publishers and unions in Sweden have found their answer in a long-term arbitration agreement. There may well be increasing reliance on this procedure.

The newspaper industry has the oldest and the firmest traditions of collective bargaining in this country. It is time to remobilize these traditions. Such remobilization could perhaps start most effectively from the early convening of national leaders of management and labor in the newspaper industry in what might be called, reflecting its purpose, a Constructive Bargaining Council.

Such a council could include the presidents of the international newspaper unions and representative publishers of comparable stature. The groundwork for the future must be laid by men with both ideas and authority.

It may be hoped that this first step would be taken by the private leaders themselves, without government—or "public"—participation. The whole idea is to develop private responsibility commensurate with private power. If the need should develop for the assistance or counsel or participation of third parties or of government offices, it can be expected that this will be requested by the parties, and will be more effective for the fact of such request.

The worst error would be to expect too much of such a council. There is no reason to believe or expect that bargaining in the newspaper industry will be put on a national basis. Every indication is to the contrary. The purpose of the council, or whatever may develop under a different name, would not even be agreement; it would be exploration of what the problems are in this industry, a free exchange of ideas and information, a spotlighting of possible new approaches and procedures.

There emerges, for example, in talking with representative and thoughtful editors, publishers, members of the press, and union leaders, a great divergence of views about the future of the newspaper industry, about the financial prospects of various kinds of newspapers, and about the future of employment needs in the different crafts. These differences appear not to be irreconcilable but to be the product rather of incomplete information. The narrowing of this area of confusion would contribute materially to the potential for responsible, farsighted collective bargaining.

There are clear signs today of the recognition on both sides of the newspaper labor relationship of the increasingly obvious axioms of automation: that the improvement of production processes cannot be held back but must be pressed to the limit; that full consideration must be given the established job rights which the new processes affect adversely; and that the accommodation of the interests of operating efficiency and employee equity demands bilateral decision-making as part of any established collective bargaining relationship.

There is no longer, if there ever was, substantial validity or vitality in the concept, at least in this industry, of annual, or biannual, thirty- or sixty-day countdown bargaining periods, separated by months or years of strained and remote undiplomatic relations restricted to the consideration of grievances involving construction or application of the old contract. The problems with which collective bargaining must deal, especially in a period of reconstruction in an industry, demand the continuing cooperative attention of the parties. The contract renewal period should come only as the culmination of an extended period of consideration of the issues which it is known will arise.

Another basic element in the newspaper collective bargaining situation is suggested by the realization that in the New York and Cleveland cases any one of the papers could have settled with any one of the unions much more easily than was possible when there were several publishers and ten unions in the picture. Any conclusion that this suggests the validity of the common editorial premise that collective bargaining should be atomized is specious. That most of the New York newspapers were not struck but were shut down voluntarily as part of a joint bargaining strategy is only one reflection of the virtual certainty that bargaining on the newspapers will proceed increasingly on a "unity" basis.

The difficulty encountered in New York does mean that the unity approach on both sides must be worked out much more constructively and effectively than it has been so far. It meant in New York that publishers and unions alike were organized to say "no" but not to say "yes." The only clearly established unity concept was the negative principle of the veto power, exercisable—and exercised—by "the majority of each one."

There is substantial agreement that the decision in New York to adopt a common expiration date for the contracts with all unions is a step in the right direction. This in itself, however, is not nearly enough. Increasing consideration will undoubtedly be given to the proposals that have already been made by some of the newspaper unions. This would contribute not only to responsible and effective collective bargaining with management, but also to the handling of the jurisdictional disputes that will develop increasingly with the introduction by more and more papers of new equipment and processes and methods.

The newspapers and the unions representing their employees have the oldest and one of the most responsible records of collective bargaining in the country. They have met crisis before. They have the capacity, the experience, the institutional structure, to meet it now. To believe deeply in the advantage of private decision-making is to feel, even against the impulse to seek a more direct course of action, that it is the appropriate function of government at this point in the collective bargaining affairs of the newspapers only to make it plain that the public expects, and will insist upon, a firmer protection of its interests than it has recently received.

If it should appear that there has been here too much of either criticism or advice, it is appropriate to reaffirm, in conclusion, complete subscription to Jefferson's view of it: that if there had to be a choice between newspapers without government or government without newspapers, the former would be infinitely to be preferred.

Fifty Years of Labor Peace*

"If you have called a bad thing bad," Goethe wrote, "you have done no great matter; but if you have called a good thing good, you have accomplished much." It is accordingly appropriate, with so much of the history of labor relations devoted to accounts of economic warfare, that a company and a union make special note of their achievement of fifty years of uninterrupted labor peace.

This story of industrial peace starts from a record of industrial war. The 1910 strike at Hart, Schaffner & Marx in Chicago was bitter and went on for many months. It would have been impossible at the time to find in the ashes of that discord the elements from which the record of that company and the Amalgamated Clothing Workers was to develop.

It is the story, essentially, of ordinary men and women, made bigger by the opportunity they seized upon.

There was Joseph Schaffner, president of the company, who stayed aloof at first, but then, when he finally became aware of the conditions which had caused the strike, said bluntly, "It should have come sooner!"—and who became, in that moment of magnanimous truth, a pioneer of twentieth-century labor-management relations.

* Amalgamated Clothing Workers Dinner Honoring the Seventy-fifth Anniversary of Hart, Schaffner & Marx, Chicago, Illinois, November 7, 1962.

There was a man on the picket line who had been an apprentice cutter for the company, and to whom an ironically perceptive foreman had said once in disgust, "A blockhead like you will never be a cutter." Sidney Hillman went on to prove the foreman right by becoming a beloved leader not just of the Amalgamated, but of all working men and women, and of all Americans.

There were the lawyers representing the company and the union, Carl Meyer and Clarence Darrow and later W. O. Thompson, who knew the meaning of Lincoln's injunction that "It is as a peacemaker that the lawyer has the superior opportunity to be a great man" and who helped write the agreement that was to be so much more than an armistice.

There was Earl Dean Howard, a professor at Northwestern University, who counseled Joseph Schaffner that labor relations are human relations, who insisted that employee complaints be fully heard and fairly adjusted, and who represented the company for many years on the arbitration board which was set up in the agreement.

There were the neutral members of that arbitration board: fair-minded, straight-spoken John E. Williams and the greatly respected James Mullenbach—trail blazers who marked out a route of industrial equity which arbitrators have followed ever since.

These names must stand for many others; and it is deliberately that this record of achievement is suggested in terms of the people who wrote it. For it is important, as the society grows larger and its economic units bigger, and as we hear more and more of machines that "think" and systems that take over, that there be no diminution or clouding of the fact that it is only people who can create whatever is new.

One possible theory would be that the relationship between Hart, Schaffner & Marx and the Amalgamated has been notable because the men who worked at it were exceptional men. There is firmer basis for the thought that they became great men at least in part because of their sharing in this experience together.

Looking back to see what else this past has to say to the future, three elements emerge most clearly.

First, these pattern-makers of collective bargaining had enough confidence in their convictions that they were willing to try for the first time measures the forces of change had made necessary.

Second, they made collective bargaining an honest process of consulting, each in good faith, the competing interests that were represented.

Third, they recognized, by their early adoption of the principle and procedure of arbitration, the need to consult, too, the public interests a neutral third person can represent.

Fifty years have only sharpened the importance of these three imperatives.

Today's architects of collective bargaining know that they must fashion new procedures which will provide retraining for people whose skills are made obsolete by new devices, that it is essential to use the new technology to the full, but that it is equally important to see that its cost is not the sacrifice and loss of job rights a man or woman has built up over years of faithful and efficient service.

Now, more than ever, it is important that there be clear recognition of the public interest in the labor relationship. There is growing sentiment that collective bargaining is not worth what it has sometimes cost in terms of strike losses, and there is increasing talk recently of the need for more government intervention to prevent strikes.

This is not a new point of view. The Department of Labor was established in 1913. One of Secretary William B. Wilson's first acts was to set up a mediation service in the new Department. It participated in sixty-two cases in 1915. Two years later the United States Conciliation Service was formally established. There were protests, and plaudits, when President Wilson intervened in the Colorado coal strike in 1914, allegedly on the side of the union. But this was as nothing compared with the crisis precipitated in 1919, when Attorney General Palmer swore out an injunction against the striking coal miners, and called out federal troops against the striking steel workers. There was also much argument in those years about "compulsory arbitration." Then, as now, there was national debate about the application of the anti-trust laws to labor unions, climaxed by the adoption in 1914 of the Clayton Act with its ringing declaration that "The labor of a human being is not a commodity or an article of commerce."

The general movement in the intervening years has been toward industrial peace. But it is not the importance of labor peace alone which is involved here. Broad public interests are affected more than they used to be by the terms of collective bargaining settlements, whether they come peacefully or after a breakdown in the process.

To look back over these past fifty years is to realize that part of their lesson is that peace came not as the goal which was sought for itself, but as the by-product of the responsible pursuit of other ends. It is the very idea of collective bargaining that there is strength and value in the free conflict between competing interests. Here, no less than in the relations between nations, those who love peace most wisely do not love it so well that they exalt it above all other ends.

What is most relevant in the story of Hart, Schaffner & Marx and the Amalgamated Clothing Workers of America is their proof that the surest guarantee against the intervention of governmental processes into the private relationship is to make the private procedures work—with voluntary enlistment, if this is necessary, of the neutral decision-making which is the essence of "public" representation. This was the central truth, the relatively simple procedure, the representatives of this company and union hit upon fifty years ago. It is an inheritance to guard and to build upon.

IV

THE PRIVATE DEMOCRACY OF LABOR

THERE WOULD BE SOMETHING WRONG, and lacking, were a Secretary of Labor not to bring to that office a full respect for the free trade union. That respect, I hope not uncritical, is undoubtedly reflected in the items in this chapter.

Yet I have been impressed most of all, during the past four years in Washington, with the realization that government is no longer administered—as it seemed to me it was when I was here twenty years ago—on a "special interest" basis, with the various Departments, of Commerce, Agriculture, and Labor, for example, pressing narrow and adversary views. This is not because there has been a change in government officials. It is because our national attitudes have changed. Private antagonisms have lessened, especially as between private institutions, and most especially as between American labor and American management. The things that unite are clearer than they used to be, and much of the underbrush of division and difference has been cleared out.

I believe it to be true, and relevant, that the last two

Secretaries of Labor, James P. Mitchell, Republican, and Arthur J. Goldberg, Democrat, contributed greatly to lifting the Department of Labor above stultifying partisanship.

To list just a few of the things American labor has stood for most strongly in the legislative debates of the past four years—the Housing Act of 1961, the Trade Expansion Act of 1962, the Vocational Education Act of 1963, the Tax Reduction Act and the Civil Rights Act in 1964—is to wonder what other group in the United States is more fully identified with the "public interest."

Labor Day*

Someplace in this park, probably in a hundred places, a little boy is tugging at his father's sleeve and whispering, "Is this going to be very long?" I was that boy forty years ago, and although my views have changed about a lot of things, they are still the same about what Labor Day is supposed to be—which is parades, picnics, and pleasure; and about what speeches are supposed to be—which is short. The answer is: "No, this isn't going to be very long at all."

In fact, my view of speeches, making them and listening to them, is that they are hard work which ought to be paid for, when performed on a holiday, at double time—and with four hours' call-in pay.

Our pride, on Labor Day, is in our heritage from those who built with their hands and their hearts the industry and the life of America. This is a sober pride, for we know the price of that heritage: that human lives were mortgaged to buy a nation's prosperity.

The storied heroes of America's phenomenal growth were industry's captains—"rugged individualists," incorporated!—who found their fortunes in the power of dollars combined in corporations, but denied the right of working men to act collectively. Theirs were the names identified with a pros-

* Barberton Joint Labor League, Fifteenth Annual Labor Day Celebration, Barberton, Ohio, September 4, 1961.

perity measured by factories that were the marvels of the world, blast furnaces that never cooled, and steel rails that pierced the farthest West.

Yet the only ultimate wealth that went into the building of the nation was labor. But labor then was an endless supply of individual men and women and children, desperate with need amid the goods they created, many so new to America they did not know even the words of protest. In a capitalism that had not found its conscience, labor was a commodity, to be bought cheaply, used up, cast aside, and replaced. America, intent on its economic balance sheet, hardly heard Ella Wheeler Wilcox, as she cried out against the human cost of it all, and caught the keynote of the nation's real economic destiny:

> O man bowed down with labor,
> O woman young yet old,
> O heart oppressed in the toiler's breast
> And crushed by the power of gold—
> Keep on with your weary battle
>   against triumphant might;
> No question is ever settled
>   until it is settled right.

We take pride in the way American labor went about winning that weary and lopsided battle, breaking history's bitter pattern of "progress" in which the glory of Egypt's pyramids was tarnished by the lives of the slaves who built them, and the roads and aqueducts of Rome were monuments to unrequited toil. Not every labor leader has been a knight in shining armor. Not every strike has been the sober voice of objective and realistic judgment. Not every picket line has waved the banners of undisputed truth. There are dark pages in the history of labor's march to economic equity.

Yet in the main, labor's way was simply to add industrial democracy to political democracy as a guarantee of freedom. Its resort was not to the bullets of rebellion or revolution, but to the ballots of union elections and to bargaining backed up by economic power.

The workers of America built the strength of their great instrument, the free trade union, out of a potent blend of practical common sense and sturdy idealism, the two most enduring factors of the American tradition. They insisted and proved that responsible unionism and constructive collective bargaining were the way to reconcile economic might and human right. Organized labor rejected, for America, any concept of progress measured by physical achievements that starve and crush the builders. It insisted that America could grow and prosper only as all the builders share in setting the terms and enjoying the fruits of their labors; that "In the human plan nothing is worth the making if it does not make the man."

So we honor on Labor Day the central American tradition: that true progress is realized only in terms of human values, and by the common decision of all who contribute to it.

If this, then, is Labor's heritage from the past, what is to be its legacy to the future? Has the battle for human values now been won?

No, nor will it ever be. The struggle of the individual for meaning is as crucial today as it has ever been.

Yet the demand upon American labor today is as new as it is old. The battle lines between the opposing forces of human and material values are different from what they were. There are new alignments, demanding new defenses, new forms of attack, new alliances—even between old antagonists—ag[illegible] [illegible]es. The ultimate collective bargain between [illegible] [illegible]ement has not been and never will be struck [illegible] [illegible]e bargaining will remain the essential demo[illegible] [illegible] arriving at decisions other nati[illegible] [illegible]e made [illegible] [illegible] of turning over to dictators [illegible] But where th[illegible] [illegible]ntral conflict was once between [illegible] [illegible]bor and American capital, it is now between [illegible] [illegible]basic forces.

[illegible], the evil that American labor faced and fought and defeated was exploitation, the taking by others of poor people's desperate toil, the crushing overuse of human beings. The "enemy" was clear. And all of labor were committed by self-interest to the struggle, for all had been the victims of economic tyranny. Today's demands upon American labor are very different. Its central cause is not that working people be protected, but that their services be used.

Once, labor's legitimate demand was for more for itself; today its needs can be met only if there is growth in the whole economy. Where, before, the call upon labor was for courage in its self-defense, the call now is for leadership in mounting an offensive on behalf of a nation bound by common economic interests.

American labor has for a century advanced freedom's cause by refusing ever to settle for the status quo, by denying that man's fate is beyond his control, by insisting that what should be can be, and that man can make it so. This is the conviction that must be pressed today, when the greatest economic need is simply that America use its full capacity, be its best self.

This is the charge upon us if we would honor faithfully those whose heritage we acknowledge on Labor Day.

The New Goals of American Labor

I have spoken at various meetings of the AFL-CIO convention several times this week, and I have heard George Meany referred to, repeatedly, as the outstanding labor leader of the world. I know that isn't enough.

By his exercise of a unique capacity to bring to American labor the strength of its unity, by his insistence that the strength of American labor be part of the strength of America, and by his taking as his personal cause the nurturing of freedom wherever it can grow in the world, George Meany has made himself the outstanding private journeyman statesman, which is the highest role that there can possibly be in a free society.

There have been so many books and articles recently about the decline and fall of labor unions in America that I came to this convention of the AFL-CIO fully prepared to attend a wake. It is my clear impression that the corpse is much more alive than the pallbearers.

It bothers me personally that most of these epitaphs have been written by men who call themselves liberals. That's my local, although I never belonged to the international. I am afraid, paraphrasing a famous epigram, that some liberals'

* AFL-CIO Fifth Constitutional Convention, New York, New York, November 14, 1963.

trouble is that they begin to complain about the conduct of labor unions when they themselves get too old to any longer set a bad example.

There has been the opportunity at the separate meetings of the AFL-CIO departments this week to listen some, and to catch again the sense of what is most on the minds of the men and women of American labor.

There has been genuine concern expressed here about civil rights, peace (and jurisdictional disputes), organizing activities, the length of work weeks, hospital insurance, wages, and a good many other things. Yet it is clear in everything that has been said, in every speech, every meeting, every other resolution, that what working people in this country are thinking about most today is, plainly and simply, *jobs.*

This is no ordinary worrying. It is a basic concern, expressed most frequently in terms of alarm about automation. Robots, mechanical men that work at wages which wouldn't feed a family, are the uninvited delegates at this convention.

There is full recognition in this hall, and among American workers, of the gains that have been made on behalf of people the last few years. There is real encouragement, in the growth of the economy these past three years, in the increase in earnings, in the rejection of the idea that depressions are inevitable. There is new evidence that a capitalism with a conscience and a government that says its business is people, and means it, can meet the challenge of technology, can break machines to the human will and purpose the way wild and powerful horses are broken.

There is, at the same time, stern insistence that the human condition is not accurately measured by seasonally adjusted decimal-point percentages, that averages can distort human truth in a society built around the central idea of equal opportunity for everybody, and that statistics must not become sedatives that soften courage into complacency and dull the national sensitivity to growing and grievous sores on the body politic. After six years of monotonous monthly reporting of unemployment at 5 percent or over, while everything else gets better, there is now a growing insistence that what is intolerable in human terms must not be permitted to become a permanent reality just because it first became a habit.

For most people, unemployment had been something happening to someone else, someplace else. Not seen first hand, there had been no real sensing of its dangers. The reported unemployment figures lost whatever shock potential they once had. Today this lethargy is lifting. What never struck home as a statistic is gradually being recognized for what it means in terms of civil rights demanded and denied, in terms of children without a future, and the remorseless advantage a machine has over an untrained man or woman. There is increasing realization that unemployment is not a low-grade fever in a distant community but a serious national virus.

Labor's central insistence is that there be a complete, unqualified commitment by the people of this country to the idea of full employment as a *first* order of business, with the clear understanding that anybody who gets in the way is going to get run over. We won our independence two centuries ago by declaring it, and meaning it. If we had started on the details first, nothing would ever have happened. We wrote a Bill of Rights in terms of our ideals, and then filled in the bill of particulars as we went along. We need this kind of commitment today.

It makes all the difference in the world whether we put truth in the first place or in the second place, and the same thing is true of full employment. We have to be concerned about the danger of inflation, but let's think about growth *first*. A balanced economic budget is important, but let's think *first* about balancing the manpower budget—at full employment. This does not mean a particular percentage. It means a job for everybody who really wants one and is able to work. It means full-time, not just part-time, jobs. It means opportunity to do work commensurate with ability, not just any job.

None of this nonsense about whether everybody who is looking for work "really needs" it. That has nothing to do with what counts in a country proud of being the land of opportunity, not just a place where people don't starve.

One of American labor's great strengths is its insistence on plain talk, on facts instead of phrases, and on human results. And so it demands, today, that the issue of full employment be debated in terms of its merits, its possibilities, its infinite promise; and not in terms of the threats and epithets of "government interference," "government spending," "unbalanced budgets," "intrusion on states' rights."

The more complicated things get, the more the advantage is with the jingoist who is willing to use a false phrase that sounds right to hurt an idea that is right. It takes patient explaining and understanding that over the long run a tax reduction leads toward a balanced budget, not a deficit, because it will mean more income for more people, more business, and even larger revenues at lower tax rates. It takes explaining and understanding that whatever is invested wisely in people, in their training and education, will be returned, with interest.

American labor rejects half-measures. It supports current programs which concentrate on the special problem of unemployment among youth, but insists properly that not many unemployed boys and girls are going to be put back to work until unemployed men and women are. Helping handicapped workers is very much worth doing, but they are the ones whose employment opportunities are most affected by a shortage of jobs. Getting dropouts to return to school is a half-measure until the necessary changes are made in what they go back to. The Manpower Development and Training Act is a landmark in social legislation, but training programs will be cruel delusions if there are not jobs at the end of them. Achieving fair employment is a half-measure unless there is also full employment.

Even though we disagree about it, you will accept the sincerity of my belief that statutory reduction of the work week would be another half-measure, because it would at best only spread unemployment, would at worst so increase costs as to curtail markets and reduce jobs, and would mean giving up the standard of living we can achieve as a nation by devoting the present work week to it.

If the primary concern of American labor today is about more jobs, it is realistic enough to recognize that full employment depends, in the age of automation, upon full education. There is great concern about how hard it is to get people who are educated and trained to see what machines are doing to people who are not educated and trained. If there are limits upon what we can do to improve the circumstances of our own generation, there is no question about our ability to remove ignorance, which is the cause of all inequality and disadvantage, from the American bloodstream.

Think what would happen in this country if we declared and waged an all-out war on ignorance. This would mean raising the standards of teachers to the levels the importance of their job demands, paying them the salaries the required skills warrant, cutting the students-to-teacher ratio to the point good sense would require, building the schoolrooms that are needed, and giving every child in the country the educational opportunity, from first grade through college, which too few have today.

Education would become our largest economic enterprise, which it ought to be. This would, in itself, go far toward creating full employment. It would wipe out ignorance. It would virtually end the intolerance and bigotry of racial and religious discrimination, rooted so deeply in ignorance. It would give young Americans the skills they need in an automated work force, and the broader knowledge a working majority of people must have if a government by the people is to make sense in a world where most of nature's forces are now being brought within human control.

Only one argument is ever advanced against this kind of war: that the cost is prohibitive. Greater than the costs of military war? Of course not. Why are the economics of a war against an alien enemy considered not only possible, but even sound, while the economics of a war against ignorance are not? If the argument is that America, with almost 10 percent of its industrial capacity lying idle and with over 5 percent of its manpower unused, is so poor that it cannot afford a war on the ignorance of its children, that argument is poppycock.

With vast unmet needs, but with limitless resources to meet them—in raw materials, in unused manpower and plant capacity, in ideas and ideals—all that stands between this nation and full employment is the determination to do what we can and must do.

American labor also demands that there be fuller provision for those who have finished their life's work. This is not just a matter of "Medicare." It is getting our thinking straight about what makes sense in life's design, and what is the basis for what we can expect of all its parts: morning, the middle hours, and the evening.

I think of Robert Frost's poem about the homeless hired man, who returned, mortally tired, to the farmhouse where he had once worked. He had in the poet's phrase, "nothing to look backward to with pride, nothing to look forward to with hope." The farmer wanted not to take him in; this was not, he said, the hired man's home. "Home," he argued, "is the place where, when you have to go there, they have to take you in." But his wife replied, "I should have called home something you somehow haven't to deserve."

More and more we are coming to the realization that the evening's peace is part, not just of the individual's earning, but of life's meaning.

Older people have become in many ways our most underprivileged minority, a universal minority to which we all seek membership, sometimes desperately. Still, as things are today, when we enter upon it, more often than not, it turns desire to disillusion and dashes hope with heartbreak. To believe deeply that life has a divine pattern is to deny the completeness of today's design of it for so many—a design which commits one of every four people over sixty-five to living alone, which denies medical aid to so many just when they need it most, deprives people of recreational opportunity just when they are free to enjoy it, faces them with stairs, literally and figuratively, just when it is hardest to climb those stairs. Too many people must spend in need and neglect what ought to be their harvest years.

Labor knows that life was not given man on terms that make it a bitter disillusionment. What failure there has been is ours, and ours to repair. It is this determination that guides the policies of American labor today. Without lessening its force as an essential agency of private bargaining, it has put its power now behind those programs that will increase the strength of the whole society, the entire economy. And so it is that labor's legislative priorities were, in 1961, a broad economic recovery program; in 1962, the Trade Expansion Act; in 1963, the tax reduction bill, the Civil Rights Act, the training and education programs, and medical care for older people. Labor's program, once, was "more" for labor; it is now "more" for people.

As we stand now at the threshold of ultimate success as an economy, labor's central insistence is on the reaffirmation of that spirit of complete national commitment which first put us in business. Its call is for a declaration of independence from want, for an economic bill of rights that starts with the right to work—in its honest sense—and for a war on ignorance and lack of preparation.

Union Morals*

The charge of corruption within the labor unions has sustained many a reformer in search of a crusade, and has given serious concern to more objective men. The evidence, so far as I know it, is that there has been neither more nor less corruption and abuse of power among (a) labor leaders, (b) bank officials, (c) corporate executives, or (d) government officials. The special emphasis which has been placed on labor union corruption reflects largely the habit of identifying shortcomings with the individual involved when he belongs to one's own club, but with the institution or group when he doesn't. If the man in the car ahead makes a left turn from the right-hand lane, he is a bad driver; but if it is a woman, she is a "woman driver."

The Landrum-Griffin Act of 1959 reflects the theory that union members are more responsible than labor leaders. The evidence is directly to the contrary, both in personal terms and with respect to collective bargaining demands. And if democracy has been declining inside some of the unions, it is more because of the members' lessening interest in union affairs than because of the occasional instances of strong-arm leadership.

* Wharton School of Finance and Commerce, Philadelphia, Pennsylvania, May 26, 1961.

As for union corruption, or racketeering, any of it is too much. A union leader stands in the position of one who has sought and won the responsibilities of trusteeship, of stewardship of other people's affairs and interests. There was enough abuse of this trust to produce the public reaction which led to the enactment of the 1959 law; and if the act illustrates the writing into the statute books of popular reactions more than of any profound policy formulations, the fact remains that this has traditionally proved to be a sound democratic process.

The record of the administration of the 1959 law reflects its vigorous enforcement. Since it became effective, 12,076 cases of alleged violations have been investigated.* Although this appears to confirm the existence of fairly widespread abuse, a breakdown of these figures offers additional illumination.

Over half of the alleged violations have been for failure to file reports required by the act, and so are properly considered as involving technical violations, in which there is no established taint of corruption. As a result, 5,459 investigations have closed by a finding that the complaint was not actionable, and 6,181 were terminated by reason of voluntary corrective action. Legal action has been required in 436 cases.

At the time the bill was being considered in Congress, some union critics charged that rank-and-file members were being denied the right to participate in their unions' democratic processes. So far, complaints regarding 915 union elections have been investigated. Violations were found in 249 elections, and 193 of these situations were remedied

* These figures have been updated as of April 1, 1964.

through voluntary action. Court actions have been necessary in 56 cases.

The significant group of cases are those involving charges of what would be considered "racketeering," such as illegal restrictions or forceful deprivation of union members' rights, embezzlement, or the holding of union office by alleged Communists or convicts. There have been 1,103 such cases since enactment of the law. In 283 of these 1,103 cases there was found to be, on investigation, supportable evidence of substantial irregularity, and in 21 of these cases voluntary compliance was obtained, usually through the international office of the union, when the irregularity was established. In 262 of these cases it has been necessary to resort to enforcement litigation. One hundred and sixty convictions have been obtained; the other cases are still in the courts.

The principal point of these figures is that the key element in the effectuation of the national labor policy to eliminate corruption in the labor movement is voluntary action within the labor movement itself. Despite some bad examples and a bad press, the fact is that most of organized labor is governed by a private democracy characterized by idealism, honesty, and responsiveness to the membership. Even in the relatively small number of cases of corruption that are brought for prosecution, there is a persistent pattern of internal responsibility. Typically, the union itself has discovered the wrongdoing of one of its members, has rectified the situation and disciplined the culprit, and has submitted the case for proceedings under the law.

If Lord Moulton's dictum was right, that "The measure of a civilization is the degree of its obedience to the unenforceable," then the labor unions of America have proved to be exceedingly civilized institutions of private democracy.

Organized Labor and the Alliance for Progress*

"Producing and disposing of the maximum quantity of consumer goods," Arnold Toynbee has pointed out, "was not the purpose of the American Revolution. What is more, it is not, of course, the true end of man." No element in our society has acted upon this principle more effectively and consistently than the American labor movement.

If there is a single purpose of American labor, that purpose is freedom. One of the hinges of the future is organized labor's increasing insistence that freedom's residence is not this country alone, or this continent, but all the world.

Time and technology have made archaic the old construct of "inter-nation" relations conducted exclusively by a small corps of formally accredited diplomats. It is with due respect for the necessary concept of national sovereignty that most of us find firmer hope for the future in the fact that the peoples of the world appear much better able to get along than do their nations. "Inter-people" relations have become the business of us all, as travelers and hosts, and in the functioning of the institutions of private as well as public government.

The common image of organized labor in this country is

* National Conference on International Economic and Social Development, Chicago, Illinois, July 19, 1962.

of a partisan, representing one set of interests against another in the competition and occasional conflict of the domestic market place. There has been too little realization of the role American labor is playing today, with extraordinary and increasing effectiveness, in world affairs—as a partisan for peace, for freedom, for human dignity.

The AFL-CIO annual budget in this area runs between one and a half and two million dollars, including hundreds of thousands of dollars to support the free trade union movement in the world (the International Confederation of Free Trade Unions), large contributions to Israel's valiant and effective Histadrut, help to Algeria's desperate workers and to many other frontiersmen of freedom. With President George Meany's special urging, the AFL-CIO has become one of the strongest and most effective private forces in the world against Communism, fighting it not just when it has attacked American institutions but wherever it has threatened free people.

Having helped greatly to achieve for the American working man the highest standard of living and the fullest measure of personal independence in the world, the American trade unions have rejected the obvious temptation of protectionism and have been effective allies in the support of the new, freer trade legislation. In this international role American labor has been guided by no self-interest except the promotion of freedom for the family of man, undivided by any line of race or religion or nationality.

Now, with the decision to mount a significant attack upon want in the Western Hemisphere, through the Alliance for Progress, the international role of organized labor assumes critical significance. One of the key structural facts the architects of the Alliance face is that the labor movement in South and Central America is powerful politically as well as economically, and is still, in many places, uncommitted on freedom's basic issues. Perón, coming to power in Argentina as a creature of the military, was quick to realize the need to build his base of support in the trade unions. When Vargas assumed power in Brazil the second time, he crushed the trade unions and then quickly created his own national labor party. Organized labor is one of the major forces of the party in control in Mexico. One of Castro's first steps was to destroy the free labor movement which had developed in Cuba, but he proceeded immediately to erect a new structure of trade unions as part of his dominion of dictatorial control.

It has by no means been true that the Latin-American trade unions have consistently proven effective bulwarks of freedom. Generalization in this respect is impossible; the record is different from country to country. In several countries there is a sharp division between free and captive labor movements. In all of them, however, there has been evidence that, given the opportunity and favorable circumstance, the labor unions will prefer to stand against dictatorial authority and on the side of people and freedom.

The fact that the labor unions constitute, throughout South and Central America, a key link between the people and their government is not being overlooked in the control centers of Communism. A United Press despatch from Mexico City in 1962 carried the announcement that "Cuba has been designated by Moscow to set up a new labor movement for the Americas to carry the Communist line throughout the New World." This is in one sense a story of Communist defeat, for this confederation was being set up because a predecessor Moscow-directed organization, with headquarters in Mexico City, had become defunct. Yet no one will miss the implications of the report that the "Fidel Castro regime has earmarked a large budget" for this new Labor Confederation of Workers of Latin America.

This reflects the need for aggressive action of the kind being carried on today by the anti-Communist Inter-American Workers Regional Organization (ORIT). It illustrates, too, the importance of such projects as the American Institute for Free Labor Development, established by the AFL-CIO, with the help of progressive businessmen in the United States and Latin-American leaders, and financed in substantial part by trade union organizations, the business community, and private foundations.

Today, as part of the Institute program, groups of trade unionists from the Central American and Caribbean countries come to the United States to participate in intensive three-month courses of study. Their training includes orientation in responsible and free trade unionism, international labor affairs and organizations, trade union organizing techniques, safeguards against threats to democratic labor, and the role of trade unions in the Alliance for Progress. When these Latin-American trade unionists return to their home countries, they work on educational and organizing programs in the unions which sponsored them, and continue to receive the benefit of their grant for an additional nine months.

It is no coincidence that wherever political democracy flourishes in the modern world there is also a strong, active, responsible, free labor movement. Latin America will be no exception. Many of the unions there are still young, still uncertain, still wavering between forces they have the strength to control, for their roots are in the people. It is of paramount importance in the success of the Alliance program to build the strongest possible bridges between the effective and free agencies of organized labor in the United States and these still uncommitted shapers of freedom's future.

Care is being taken to assure against trying to shape the Alliance program in the mold of our own experience. It is essential that we see the problems and goals of our allies through their eyes, not our own. There are, at the same time, close parallels between our experience and theirs.

I think, in this connection, of a conversation with an exceedingly thoughtful and articulate young man who had just come to Washington from one of the newly invigorated Central American republics. He had been in the labor movement in his country before entering its government. After we had talked for a time I expressed some surprise at his familiarity with the story of the development of the American labor movement. He replied, as nearly as I can reconstruct his words: "Yes, I do know this story. This is partly because we identify our present situation as a country, and our hopes for it, with what American working people faced seventy-five or a hundred years ago, and what they have accomplished since that time." When I pressed him as to what he considered the most significant of our accomplishments and his hopes, he answered with a smile, borrowing his phrase from another piece of history, "Equality. Fraternity. Liberty."

Against the background of American labor experience and history, it is apparent that two elements in the blueprint of Bogotá and in the charter of Punta del Este represent comparative innovations in the architecture of inter-people relations. One is that to try to shape economic progress without equal attention to social development is to make bricks without straw. The other is that the lasting quality of whatever progress is made will be measured by the mutuality of participation which goes into it.

It is said repeatedly that South and Central America are on the eve of an "industrial revolution." That phrase marks, in the minds of Americans who know our own history well, the unnecessarily bitter lesson of economic progress without social development. How grand a thing it will be if, as we turn to help these tens of millions of people on the Andes' slopes push out of the past into the modern world, we also help spare them the price our own industrial revolution cost us—in terms of lives that were needlessly ground, so far as the meaning of living was concerned, into the new machines, and in terms of gains that were distributed with gross inequity.

The architects and administrators of the Alliance will face inevitably the pressures of those who will demand the most obvious manifestations of economic progress. Insecure governments will grab at opportunities to build monuments people can see; and it is a central policy of the Kremlin to capitalize on this impatience for economic progress. We must move quickly to meet these forces.

Surely America has learned its lesson about the unseemly and ineffective business of chasing around the world with checkbooks, trying to outbid the offer of Soviet mercenaries, putting unintended but inevitable pressure on our best friends to blackmail us, forgetting that our money is no more attractive than the Russians', and wasting the advantage we do have, which is that we can help build mansions for the soul as well as dams and steel mills.

It is the essential democratic conviction, distinguishing it from the Communist ideology, that any organized attempt to improve mankind's lot is not worth the doing just to satisfy men's appetites but only as it serves also their social purpose. We know that in people's desires hunger speaks louder than hope, yet there need be no choice made between economic and social development. In his Inaugural Address, in 1949, as the first elected Governor of Puerto Rico, Luis Muñoz Marín said, in the authentic voice of those in want:

> A political status . . . does not exist in an economic vacuum. . . . If a community does not develop an economy which is founded, or has hopes of being founded, on a victorious productive effort, it will see other forms of its life and liberty impeded, or decayed, or destroyed. . . . It is not a mere material convenience to be free from want.

Yet he asserted "above all" the need even an impoverished people have for "a high ideal of the spirit," a readiness and a desire "to create an understanding of deep and clean human fraternity . . . to give root to attitudes that lead man to be more creative than acquisitive . . . and to destroy bitterness of race, language, and culture."

The Alliance will serve its purposes only as we can associate ourselves not just with our neighbors' wants and fears, but more with their hopes and their ideals. It is not satellites but associates we seek in this new hemispheric enterprise. When we say "allies" we must mean it in the full sense of mutuality the term implies. Our purpose is not to get these nations "on our side." It is rather to help them be vigorously and intelligently on the side of their own freedom and integrity.

Let us be quite open, furthermore, in our recognition that we need allies for the future as much as they need us. For the fact is that the republics of South and Central America must emerge from their present transition dedicated to some form of freedom's principle if democracy as we know it is to continue to exist.

V

DISCRIMINATION AND DISADVANTAGE

THE "RACIAL PROBLEM" has been a matter of acute national concern at least since the school desegregation cases in 1954. The Civil Rights Acts of 1957 and 1960 were mileposts of progress, but "deliberate speed" had become too deliberate by 1963. Suddenly the attention and conscience of Americans were seized by those who demanded freedom and equality *now*. The time for truth had come, and so had the time for law.

It was also time to recognize, however, the relevance of Goldsmith's admonition:

> How small, of all that human hearts endure,
> That part which laws or kings can cause or cure!

For even a successful attack on discrimination will yield only a beachhead on the shores of disadvantage. Even with the enactment of the Civil Rights Act of 1964, the hardest part of the job still lies ahead.

The major battle which must be fought on the way to the

Great Society is the war against the evils of poverty: the rotting slum, the barren farm, and, most of all, the blighted child. Hopefully, the civil rights movement, concerned as it is with unqualified people as well as with qualified Negroes, will become a major force in this battle.

There are those who say that we cannot afford to pass on debts to our children. It seems to me the debts we most clearly cannot afford to pass on to our children are the debts of ignorance, of disease, of juvenile delinquency. Instead, we must bequeath to each child the full promise of America —a land where every individual can find as complete expression and satisfaction in life as his talents and energies make possible. Woodrow Wilson said once that we must believe what we tell our children. I would add that we must also give them the chance to practice what we preach.

An Affirmative Equal Employment Opportunity Program*

A time comes in the pursuit of any worthwhile purpose when the value of what is said about it depreciates and then disappears. Equal opportunity is obviously such a purpose, and a hundred years after the Emancipation Proclamation and ten years after the Supreme Court decision in *Brown* vs. *Board of Education* is such a time. The value of words is wearing out.

In too large part, these years of the century and the decade have been years of discouragement, of the frustration of repeated new promise. In the past ten years, numerous nations have entered the council of world society through membership in the United Nations; and their citizens, most of them with the sun in their skin, have found new dignity in their lives. Yet there has seemed to be little change in the meaning of being a Negro in America. Each year of this decade has seen new miracles wrought in the nation's laboratories. New truths in the science of things have been disclosed. Yet the central, simple truth in the science of people, that all people are created equal, has stayed too much on people's tongues and not entered into the bloodstream of

* Regional Conference, President's Committee on Equal Employment Opportunity, Chicago, Illinois, May 22, 1964.

their honest conviction. The gateways of space have opened wider in the last ten years than have the doorways of some schools.

Now the time for truth, the human truth, the truth of deeds and not words, has come. The Negro citizens of this nation have taken their stand. They will not be moved and they ought not be moved. It is rather for the rest of America to respond—in deeds, not words. There is no need to rephrase our purpose or to repeat our pledges. The response now must be in terms of doing. We can do the right thing or we can do the wrong thing, but the choice of doing nothing has disappeared forever.

The Civil Rights Act of 1964 will mean a virtual end to overt acts of discrimination in hiring. Yet we know that equal employment opportunity requires a great deal more than that.

President Johnson noted at Wayne State University in 1963 the limited effectiveness in this area even of monumental official action. He said of the Emancipation Proclamation, "While we in America have freed the slave of his chains, we have not freed his heirs of their color. Until Justice is blind to color, until education is unaware of race, until opportunity ceases to squint its eyes at pigmentation of human complexion, Emancipation will be a Proclamation but it will not be a fact."

The Emancipation Proclamation established the legal equality of the Negro in America. But it was not accompanied by the economic and social measures which would give reality to that position. So it was not enough. It was half a social revolution, and for lack of the other half was in truth no revolution at all. Before that time a high economic wall had been built around the Negro, and the whites had said to him, "You can't get out." But after that time the whites built a high economic wall around themselves and said to the Negro, "You can't get in."

The Civil Rights Act will mean a great deal, but like the Proclamation it will leave a very great deal to be done. We dare not today, in the process of finally effectuating civil rights, overlook the economic rights which alone give meaning to legal equality. The plain fact is that freedom and groceries are both important, and neither is enough without the other.

I think of three boys leaving their homes in Chicago's South Side in the morning to look for work. One finds a job vacancy, but it is denied him in an act of sheer and unadulterated bigotry. A second finds a job opening too, but is turned away because he lacks a high school diploma. He "dropped out." The third boy looks all day for a job, and can't find one. Then there is a fourth boy, who didn't look for work that morning at all, but stayed home in bed, sleeping away the effects of a misspent night.

The problems we face in these cases are not going to be met adequately with pity or sentimentality. Two of those four boys deserve more sympathy than the other two. Yet as far as the concerns of the community go, as far as the public interest which is involved here is important, all four boys require the most serious attention we can possibly give them. Only one of the four is even touched by the Civil Rights Act of 1964.

Civil rights have got to include rights that satisfy the needs of people's arms and stomachs as well as the need of their ears. The right to work, in the sense of there being a job available, is an essential right. So is the right to be ready, for the jobs that are and will be available.

Columnist James Reston, measuring the progress and problems of these ten years after the school desegregation case, has commented that the Negro in America "is gaining legally but is falling behind economically. He's slowly getting the rights but not the skills of a modern computerized society. He's getting a better chance at skilled jobs, but unskilled jobs are being wiped out by the new Boss Man, the Machine." Then Reston added, "No doubt this ironical situation will pass in time."

It will take more than time. This situation will pass only as there is developed a program of affirmative action to back up the prohibitions and the restraints of the Civil Rights Act.

Reston went on, "One of the tragedies of the Abolitionists of 100 years ago is that they spent all of their energy on the legal abolition of slavery and did little to plan for the realities of victory." It is time now to plan for the realities of victory.

So far as equal employment opportunity is concerned, civil rights will become real in this country only as there is developed a three-point program of civil responsibility.

First, there must be more total opportunity created, more jobs. Fair unemployment is no good; the only thing that is important is fair employment, which will come as part of full employment.

Second, equal employment opportunity will be meaningless except as there is real equality of educational and training opportunities.

Third, local equal opportunity programs must be developed within every disadvantaged community. They must be developed not by outsiders but by the members of that community, and they must include the rebuilding of the whole structure of life and attitude in that community.

Equal opportunity depends today upon much more than simply changing some rules. It is not essentially a matter of stopping something. It is a matter of starting and continuing affirmative action. It requires—and we must face it in its full dimension—the restructuring, the revitalizing, of large segments of the American economic and social structure.

The first of the three points, the need for more jobs, should be clearly understood. The equity of equal opportunity is obviously just as great where there is unemployment as where there is full employment. Unemployment is no excuse for any kind of discrimination. Yet it remains a clear, pragmatic fact that guaranteeing equal employment opportunity will be doubly difficult when providing opportunity to one person means taking it away from another. So, until the economy as a whole is invigorated and more jobs created, our success in equalizing employment opportunity is going to be at best partial and incomplete.

The importance of educational and training opportunity as a foundation of equality of employment opportunity cannot be overstated. The achievement of true equality of employment opportunity will, in my judgment, be seriously retarded by the adoption of any even temporary policy of giving hiring preference to any less qualified person over one who is better qualified. Yet there should be an affirmative obligation on employers, on labor unions, and on the community as a whole to counteract the inequality which has developed in connection with the various educational and training programs, including apprenticeship programs.

If an employer or a labor union has in the past discriminated against applicants for jobs or membership on the basis of race, it is not enough for that employer or for that union simply to stop discriminating. There is an affirmative responsibility to counteract the effect of the previous policy. This does not mean hiring or admitting unqualified applicants. It does mean making it clear that the old policy has been changed, and participating in the preparation and training of people who would have been ready if it had not been for that previous discrimination. It also means accepting when they are ready those who would have been accepted earlier if there had not been a discriminatory policy.

As we move into the affirmative stages of the Equal Opportunity program, it will be all to the good to recognize that in many respects it is not basically a race or minority group problem. A disproportionate number of minority group members are unemployed today, but our inquiries reveal more and more clearly the closer correlation between unemployment and the lack of education than between unemployment and the race of the individuals involved.

The 1960 census figures for Chicago illustrate this. The highest unemployment rate in the city that year, a shocking 35.5 percent—compared with a national rate (for men) of 5.2 percent—was in census tract No. 543 (between 26th and 31st Streets and Indiana Avenue and State Street). The population there was 97 percent Negro.

But in another census tract (No. 682-Z, running east of State Street, south of 95th Street, east of Harlan High School) in which the population was 96 percent Negro, the unemployment rate was 2.6 percent, which was only half the national average.

The real difference between these two census tracts had

nothing to do with race. It is rather the fact that in the first census tract the median educational attainment level was only eight years—two years *below* the city-wide average—and in the second census tract, the median educational attainment rate was two years *above* the city-wide average.

A broader review of other areas in Chicago and in other cities reveals this dominating and repetitious pattern: unemployment is associated again and again with low educational attainment. This is not just a racial problem, a problem of unequal employment opportunity resulting from marks upon a people's skin; it is a matter of unequal employment opportunity resulting in significant part from the lack of educational opportunity either in this generation or in those which have come before.

People ask repeatedly how many of these with whom we are dealing are educable? There is only one answer to that: every single one of them. We won't measure up to that goal of accomplishment, but we can come infinitely closer to it than people realize.

Some ask, "How many of these people who have dropped out of school and are now standing around on street corners want an education?" In November of 1963, we interviewed 2,500 boys who had failed to pass the Armed Forces Qualification Test. Among those who had failed because of lack of educational attainment, 55 percent came from broken homes. Most of them came from parents who had less than a grade school education. Most of the boys had themselves dropped out of school. When we asked them whether they would be willing to go back, either for occupational training or for basic education of one kind or another, the answers were affirmative in over 85 percent of the cases. Interestingly enough, the percentage of affirmative answers from the Negro boys was five points above the affirmative answers from the white boys.

The necessary third element in an affirmative Equal Employment Opportunity program is the development of an essentially local community rehabilitation program which includes a complete remolding of community structures and attitudes. The Woodlawn project in Chicago and the HARYOU and ACT projects in Harlem have features which are subject to legitimate differences of opinion, but those who are developing these programs are unquestionably right in their central insistence that any community reconstruction program has to be developed from within the community if it is to have lasting significance. There is a role in these programs for outsiders, often a critical role, particularly at the early stages. But unless a complete self-sufficiency is developed, the weakness of "welfare colonialism" is bound to emerge.

The necessity of this inner direction derives principally from the fact that the roots of the problem, poverty and unemployment and lack of education, go so deep. No amount of outside administration will change this root structure. The change will come only as there is a remolding of the thinking and of the living patterns of the people who are the community involved.

Is there time for the job which needs to be done? Yes. Doubts about this come principally from the fact that most of the reports we hear are of those cases in which somebody is falling behind. The four major problems in the world may be viewed in terms of four sets of difficult relationships: between nations; between men and machines; between labor and management; and between the races. Daily newspaper reports make all of these issues appear insoluble, and worsening. Yet those who know these problems closely know that great advances are being made from day to day, and that even if there is a logic to suggest that these problems cannot be met in time, the facts are that they will be.

This is not just a protestation of faith. It becomes increasingly clear that the great majority of people in this country, and in the world, want to find their meaning in something more than the development of their own individual lives. The basic desire is to find the sense of things in improving life as a whole by adding dignity and meaning to other people's lives.

We must not be distracted or discouraged by the noise of the occasional incident. A great deal is being accomplished. There is time—for everything except doing nothing. There is time to seize the opportunity presented by the gains we have made and to build from there to the end we have in mind.

To move along in life is to feel increasingly people's deep desire to help bequeath to their children a nation in which none of them is robbed by men of the gifts God gave him, in which any disadvantage he is heir to is not increased but is diminished by life's events, and in which every person is valued not by any mark of any kind upon his body but by what is within him. Such a nation will have the kind of strength that endures, and it will be a model and magnet of hope to the entire world.

Fair Employment and Full Employment*

The fair employment practices issue is misconceived when it is thought of in terms of an American worker's saying, or thinking, "I don't want anyone of a different race working with me." What is much more likely is his saying, "I don't want *anybody* to get *my* job." I think there would be in this country today almost complete acceptance in practice of the fair employment principle if there were in fact full employment.

Consideration of the matter of equal employment opportunity can be helpfully prefaced by reference to the seemingly unrelated matter of work stoppages at the missile sites. In 1961 there was strong public criticism of such stoppages. A serious problem had unquestionably developed. But the criticism far exceeded the cause. It dealt unfairly with the position of the unions involved.

After several rounds of public attack and counterattack which accomplished nothing, at least in themselves, the missile sites problem was taken up quietly by reasonable and responsible men who considered, patiently, the specific problems and cases involved. The results of their efforts are reflected in the Second Annual Report of the Missile Sites

* Building and Construction Trades Department Convention, New York, New York, November 7, 1963.

Labor Commission, covering the period from June 1962 to June 1963. This report shows only one man-day lost because of a labor dispute for every 1,288 man-days worked; 99.92 percent of all available work time on missile sites entirely free of work stoppages; every missile site finished and ready on schedule to receive weapons and crews. This is a proud record of private and public cooperation based entirely on the exercise of private responsibility, with no exercise of public "power."

Today there is comparable concentration of public attention on the practices of the building and construction trades with respect to the employment of the minority group members, especially Negroes. Here again there is unquestionably a problem. Here again there are sharp criticism and sharp reply, which are presently contributing nothing to improving the situation. Here too, however, responsible men are now sitting down together and talking quietly and dispassionately about particular parts of this problem and what to do about it.

Representatives of the Building and Construction Trades Department and of its constituent unions have criticized sharply and strongly some elements of the Labor Department's position regarding this matter. Thank heaven for the frankness of these expressions, and for what the freedom to criticize implies about this system of ours. You will expect equal frankness from me, solely in the interests of reaching that understanding which we all know can and will be found.

I do not think of this, incidentally, as a matter of trying or being able to "satisfy" everybody or even anybody. There was one day last month when two documents came to my desk, almost simultaneously, relating to the administration of the Labor Department's apprenticeship program. One was the public statement of a respected general president of one of the building and construction trade unions. It protested bitterly the steps which have been taken in the Department of Labor to make it clear that this statutory program will not be used to promote discriminatory apprenticeship plans. These steps were condemned as "government pressures and dictation," and the work of "social experimenters" and "impractical reformers." The report ended up with the admonition "Hands off!" The other document was a decision and opinion by a respected federal judge. Talking about exactly the same situation, the judge criticized the Labor Department's Bureau of Apprenticeship and Training for its "overall apathy," and for "passively assisting and aiding" in the perpetuation of discriminatory practices. It was like getting a ticket for speeding and illegal parking at the same time.

I hope it will help if I state as plainly as I can what seem to me the key facts in this situation.

It is important beyond everything else that there is complete agreement about the central issue of principle which is involved. On June 21, 1963, the presidents of the international unions affiliated with the Building and Construction Trades Department issued a policy statement affirming unequivocally the position that with respect to union membership, hiring lists, referral systems, and apprenticeship programs, the policy of the Department and of these international unions is that there will be no discrimination on the basis of race, creed, color, or national origin.

I have said before Congressional committees, and in some public meetings where it was not popular to say it, that this statement is entitled to full respect as the honest statement of honorable men. Those who deny it this respect are wrong, and they make a serious mistake in discounting the essential fact that the meaningful policy of the AFL-CIO and of the Building and Construction Trades Department is that there should be complete equality of employment opportunity.

The real issues—and they are important and serious issues—are about what may be reasonably expected in implementing this policy, and about what the role of government should be where there are departures from it.

It is important and meaningful that the American labor movement, no less than the civil rights groups, and along with the administration, supports vigorously and without reservation Federal Fair Employment Practices legislation.

It is also essential that it be recognized that many of the criticisms of the building and construction trades' membership policies have been grievously unfair, in their generalization, to those unions which have either traditionally or more recently eliminated every vestige of racial discrimination. It has hurt that so serious a matter is being debated and argued, on both sides, in terms of badly aimed broadsides that do more to alienate allies than to weaken the opposition. I hope earnestly that very soon we will reach that point where the spokesmen on all sides of this issue can concentrate on speaking to each other instead of to their own constituents.

I also urged recognition of what I think are fair protests against the slow rate of progress in implementing the policies that have been adopted, and fair objections to some of the positions that have been taken in defense of the present situation.

There are two large building trades locals in New York City, with a total membership of about 4,500, which have no

Negro members. A question exists as to whether another local with a membership of 3,300 has any Negro members. There are comparable situations in many other cities. In too many locals the announced policy of this Department and of the international unions is not a reality in fact.

A survey of federal construction projects in some fifty cities, conducted in the summer of 1963, showed that on most of these projects there were no Negroes employed in a majority of the skilled trades, either as journeymen or as apprentices. It is no answer to this that a comparable situation exists in skilled occupations in other industries. We face, as a nation, the obligation to correct an acknowledged wrong; and a clear consensus has been reached that we are going to do it.

The important questions are of ways and means. Some proposed short cuts are, as most of us view it, wrong. It is clear that quotas are wrong. No one in government has proposed them. It is clear that the opening of trades and apprenticeship programs to all alike, without regard to their race, in no way implies or warrants reducing the skill levels of the crafts.

There is argument about whether preferential hiring of Negroes, to counteract the effect of previous discrimination against them, is now in order. I think it is not, if for no other reason than that such a policy will, as a practical matter, create opposition which will retard the over-all process.

I am equally clear, however, that where there are apprenticeship lists that contain no Negroes because they knew they didn't have a chance, those lists should be opened up on a fair basis. The argument that it is "just too bad" if Negroes did not apply is not a fair argument. It is also a false argument to claim that this will prevent the following of father-and-son practices that have a justification, for there are few if any situations in which the necessary adjustments cannot be made to serve all interests involved if there is the sincere purpose to do so.

There has been the suggestion that the government's program for promoting sound apprenticeship systems cannot properly be used to foster nondiscriminatory programs, and there is criticism of our insistence that federal construction projects be carried out on an equal-opportunity basis. Yet it must be recognized, as a matter not only of law but of fundamental principle, that the government is the agent of *all* Americans and cannot properly favor any above any others.

The nation is faced today with the proper and overdue demand of a substantial group of its members for full participation in our economy and with the need to promote this full participation for our common betterment. What is required to meet this demand and need is simply that a man be hired on a job, or given his opportunity for apprenticeship, or for membership in a union, with no regard whatsoever to the fact of his race. The only real question is whether prior practices of one kind or another, some of them with other justifications, are to stand in the way of honoring this clear-cut principle. The judgment of the nation and of the trade union movement is that this principle is paramount.

The Mountain Called Disadvantage*

Sitting last evening at my desk at home, beneath a picture of the original author of Equal Opportunity Day, I found myself repeating his grandly simple reminder that "all men are created equal," and then looking up and asking, "Are they?"

In what meaningful sense are all men created equal?

Lincoln spoke directly to the error that had developed in a nation's thinking: that in the act of creation itself there was an intended distinction which was marked by the color put in children's skins. Until that false notion was corrected nothing could be accomplished.

Today, too long a century later, that earlier ignorance has been substantially overcome. If there is not yet unanimity in the nation, there is nevertheless a clear consensus that accords with our conscience. Americans are agreed now that life was not designed in the pattern of discrimination. Yet there is much more to it than this, and what lies ahead requires something beyond the recognition of a divine equity.

It is as though in this historic hundredth year we had climbed a mountain, called Discrimination, only to find on approaching the summit that what lies ahead is another

* Washington Urban League's Equal Opportunity Day Committee's 1963 Observance, Washington, D.C., November 18, 1963.

mountain, called Disadvantage. If the error in men's minds a century ago warranted the reminder that "all men are created equal," the necessity today is that America face squarely the limitations within which this is true. For the fact is that each boy or girl brings with him very different gifts from God, and that with his first breath a child's endowment becomes principally whatever portion of advantage or disadvantage the circumstances of his environment confer upon him.

In the century ahead, the requirement upon America is that it be dedicated to the proposition that men will correct the inequalities that men have created. The inequities children inherit must be lifted from them. Equal opportunity today must include much more than freedom from denial of opportunity when the chance comes. If equal opportunity is to mean anything, it must include the right to be ready.

The equal right to work is perhaps closest to the surface, if not the heart, of a great many of today's long overdue demands, and it presents some of the hardest problems.

There will be loss, not gain, from any person's demanding or receiving a job for which he is not qualified. Honest and sincere men reach different conclusions about whether previous discrimination warrants preference now, to "even things up." My own strongly held view is that such preference could be justified only on an assumption that this is a matter of competition between two sides. It is not, and there is great importance in avoiding and eliminating any mistaken grouping along color lines. The victims of preference would be individual human beings, and, more likely than not today, persons who are themselves opposed to discrimination. To think in terms of quotas is again to think in terms of two groups, which is to be avoided. Federal Fair Employment Practices legislation is essential, and this law must be administered in terms of the absolute of equality, with no exceptions of any kind.

To believe in equality of opportunity except as it increases competition for one's own job is selfish hypocrisy. Discrimination is no less ugly for its being inspired by self-interest, entirely unrelated to racial prejudice.

Yet "more than equality" is not only justified, but is required so far as preparation for opportunity is concerned. There is no unfair hurting of someone else if preference in education is accorded those who have been previously disadvantaged. Here there is only the necessary neutralizing of the ravages of a century of unfairness. Surely the single most critical front in the current battle for meaningful equal opportunity is the education of the presently disadvantaged minority group youth.

Actually, this minority can be best described not in racial terms at all but in terms of all disadvantaged youth. We hate the bigotry of racial prejudice with all that is in us, especially when it is inflicted on a child. But the hurt to a child is no less when he is denied a fair chance for any reason beyond his control. Racial discrimination is no worse in its effect than the discrimination which results from poverty, from chronic unemployment, from growing up in a slum. The poet Alfred Lord Tennyson said it: "Cursed be the social wants that sin against the strength of youth."

It is not enough today to be against discrimination. That is easy now. If we are to be true to ourselves, we will buckle down to the job of preparing the next generation to seize opportunities they do not (because they cannot) know they have. We have effectively opposed the folly of discrimination. Now we must stop the fallout of disadvantage. We must get through to these boys and girls that there is opportunity beyond what they have seen at home.

If we believe what we say, we will put our best schools in the slums, not in the suburbs.

If we believe what we say, we will make a flat commitment to *all* American boys and girls that they will receive all the education they are willing to use, right on through college.

Equal opportunity will not come merely by preventing the denial of opportunity to those disadvantaged by reason of race or previous condition of environment. Equal opportunity will come only by giving those who are at least ready for opportunity the preparation they need. "It is here," it has been said, "that more than equality makes sense; and today anything less makes no sense at all."

"A nation conceived in liberty and dedicated to the proposition that all men are created equal." What Lincoln was saying, of course, was that what fault there is, what inequality, is not of God's making, but of man's, and that it is man's to correct.

A National Commitment to Youth*

The tendency to decry the younger generation has been properly diagnosed as a form of mental arthritis for which there is no known cure. Why, indeed, should there be so much concern about youth unemployment at a time when a dozen statistical measures confirm the fact that the current edition of American youth faces *on the average* a brighter future than any preceding generation of inhabitants of any known region of the universe?

The short answer lies in the dangerous inadequacy of averages when they are applied to people who are members of a society whose central idea is equality for everybody. The ideas of equality and "the average" are enemies to each other. Equality is a magnificent absolute. There is no legitimate contentment in the comfortable condition of the majority. This free society can furnish full and equal opportunity to every one of its members. Its doing so is the only true measure of its success. No averaging of statistics should be permitted to camouflage the fact that between five and ten million American boys and girls between the ages of sixteen and twenty today face futures they are not prepared for, and won't be unless something is done about it.

---

* National Committee on Employment of Youth, Washington, D.C., November 6, 1963.

Unemployment is today the infantile paralysis of the economy, striking down teen-agers at three times the rate it attacks adults. It must be treated as the epidemic it has become.

This crisis has developed with comparative suddenness. The technological revolution on the farms in the fifties sent a flood tide of boys and girls from the country to the city; only one of ten growing up in a rural area today will stay there. Now the postwar birth bomb has hit the work force, with 900,000 more boys and girls reaching the age of sixteen in 1963 than in 1962. With automation spreading now through the production and service trades, the proportion of jobs open to new and untrained workers is dropping rapidly. What the nation could not realize in terms of increasing youth unemployment it is now sensing fully in terms of worsening juvenile delinquency, the fallout from unemployment.

Suddenly alarmed, we have started pushing panic buttons. One is marked "dropouts." In the spring and summer of 1963, there was set in motion a nationwide program of getting the dropouts back into school. The National Education Association mounted an all-out, person-to-person effort. Someone started up Dropouts Anonymous. We all took part in fund-raising rallies of one kind or another, and exhorted these refugees from reality, as we know it, to come back.

The NEA has issued a report on the results of this nationwide campaign: over half a million boys and girls dropped out of school during the first six months of the year; about 75,000 of them, or one in eight, were persuaded to return in the fall; and it is estimated that nine out of ten of those who came back dropped out again within six months. Too many of them saw their older brothers out of jobs, even though they had completed high school, because there are not enough jobs to be had. Others found their schools still overcrowded and still not geared to train them for jobs that are available. The total salvage was perhaps 7,500 or 10,000 young people.

It was worth it, both in terms of the individual futures reclaimed and for what the effort showed of people's willingness to be ashamed, to get mad at themselves, and to do something about an outrageous human failure.

But it is plain that this kind of "humanized" approach, important as it is, is not enough. There is so much more involved here than just keeping boys and girls from stumbling, from making mistakes, from quitting. The "dropout" isn't the trouble; he is a symptom. So is the juvenile delinquent—at an advanced stage.

If we mean business about reducing—yes, eliminating—youth unemployment, it should be made clear what is involved. It isn't a job for summer patriots. It means strengthening the whole economy. It means performing surgery on the educational system. It means breaking the cycle of hereditary poverty, and of second- and third-generation unemployment and ignorance. It means taking stern emergency measures immediately to prevent wholesale disaster from hitting even while these other, more basic answers are being worked out. It means a national commitment to American youth—a commitment to prepare every young American for a job and to develop jobs for every American.

There must be realistic recognition that any improved educational or training or rehabilitation program will be a delusion and a deception unless there are job opportunities at the end of it. The President's Committee on Youth Employment noted at the outset of its report that "Underlying all efforts to help youth is the need for expansion of the economy."

This leaves the equally real fact that as matters now stand there is an accumulating body of young Americans who are not only unemployed but who are not prepared, and are not going to be prepared, for the kind of jobs which even an invigorated economy will open up to them.

In only one area is there yet anything like a complete awakening to this situation. It may well prove to be the larger result of this year's civil rights advance that it becomes recognized that the most meaningful minority group in this country is the group, regardless of race or creed or color, which is denied the educational and training opportunity which is accorded the majority.

We are approaching the point where the key element in what we call racial discrimination is the denial of motivation to the child of poverty. It is not lack of ability. If there was inequality of opportunity before—and there was—this inequality is being rapidly reduced. What remains is primarily that form of discrimination, or disadvantage, which puts him at his desk in the first grade with no more motivation than what he brings from a home which has been blighted by discrimination.

Distressingly large numbers of boys and girls are isolated, more dangerously than we realize, from the healthy society we know. A boy whose father has not been able to support his family thinks of welfare payments and unemployment compensation as a way of life. He actually knows nothing of what work really is, or nothing at least of the dignity and satisfaction of it.

We don't know how to speak to these youth. As our experience in life has not been theirs, so neither are our language nor our customs, nor our dress, nor our goals theirs. So many of these young Americans simply do not know, today, the opportunities they have. This is the point of the Widening Horizons program which the wives of the last two Secretaries of Labor and a number of other women have been promoting here in Washington the past two years. Some way has to be found to make these young boys and girls look up instead of down.

The person who is best able to stop the minority group inheritance of poverty and ignorance is the teacher. She can take the boy or girl who comes into her classroom knowing no reason to try, because life at home offers no reason, and give that handicapped child the motivation which the American majority has as its birthright. But this won't happen in classrooms in which one teacher faces forty children, and works through a course of study based on the fallacious assumption that they are all going on to college. Today's educational system is designed for winners, and it ignores losers, partly because we don't like to admit there are losers in our society.

The dropouts could well cry out with Browning, in half-truth: "O Lord, make no more giants, but elevate the human race."

It is an important part of the national philosophy in this country that all useful work has intrinsic dignity. We must guard against any assumption that only professional, white-collar, and skilled jobs are worth educating for.

Educators and those involved in labor market operations face a critical need for the development of carefully integrated programs for the fruitful training of all different kinds of youngsters for all different kinds of productive, constructive lives.

It will not help just to chain reluctant learners to desks that do not interest them. The answer is obviously not to lower educational standards so that more students can and will stay in school longer. The need is for much more, of course, than the expansion of vocational education facilities.

I hope that eventually the only special programs which will be necessary to supplement the general education system will be retraining programs for those who need such retraining when they have to change jobs. In a properly functioning economy it ought to be possible for even most of the retraining jobs to be done privately. But we are not at that point today.

Passage of the Youth Employment Act or its equivalent is essential to the meeting of the situation we presently face. Through it, over a quarter of a million boys will serve in the Youth Conservation Corps during its first five years. Each boy will have from six months to two years of an experience providing the environment and the leadership to counteract the effect of an inheritance of poverty or discrimination and the acquired characteristics of days and nights roaming the streets. The effects of poverty and social alienation can be neutralized by removing boys from the deathlike vise of their environment, and giving them an active, orderly, and democratic life under the influence and leadership of concerned and dedicated men who like youth and take pride in their work.

The effects of educational deprivation can be met, at least in part, by programs of specially developed instruction at whatever level a boy may require, from first grade to high school.

The YCC will constitute one of the most exciting educational opportunities of our day. We are going to find out how to teach reading to a twenty-year-old who is illiterate, ashamed of his ignorance, and determined not to reveal it. The YCC intends to experiment and research every reasonable hypothesis in this relatively new area of teaching. What the YCC learns, we shall share, and the nation will profit by it.

The Neighborhood Youth Corps will, in addition, provide over sixty thousand jobs for young men and women in its first year and more than a half-million over a five-year period. This will be not only a massive atack but also a flexible one, because its projects will be locally conceived and operated.

Beyond learning a skill and developing work habits, young people employed in such projects will assume a new role in their communities. They will gain new respect in their families and the opportunity to break away from the idle crowd. At least they will have good reason to get up in the morning as we do and to be tired at night and sleep when we do. They can begin to think in a realistic way about next steps—about further training and education as a means to a vocational goal, about marriage and a family they can support.

We need unity of purpose among those who have jobs for youth, those who find jobs for youth, and those who know youth best. Employers must learn what these youth are like, how to work with and for them, and why their development of jobs for youth is in the national interest as well as their own. The social agencies must learn what the realities of the job market are now and can be expected to be in the future so they can see the dimensions of the job of preparing youth for these realities.

The schools must learn what the job market requires of education and what the lives of these young people will demand. They must apply this knowledge with a new depth of understanding of their students' problems and in new techniques of teaching. The employment services must learn what new organizational devices and counseling techniques will be required of them to speed their conversion from a capable placement agency serving skilled workers to a service with a major emphasis on putting unskilled youth on the road to productive employment.

With this knowledge we can mold community resources into a coordinated service for the employment of youth—one system that uses the skills of the employment counselor, the psychologist, the minister, the detached worker, the recreation specialist, and the teacher.

The starting point must be a national commitment to youth, an appeal to and a response from the conscience and the heart of every American.

The Opportunity to Be Equal*

The Economic Opportunities, or Anti-Poverty, Bill says that our belief in progress includes the conviction that there are to be no human hostages to progress.

The purpose of government in a democracy must be indistinguishable from the purpose of those who are its members. To the extent that our lives as individuals find their meaning in what we can add to the lives of others, a program to fight poverty is the embodiment of the central ideal of this system of government. It seeks to assure that every American has the opportunity to be equal. The text for this legislation could well be: "Inasmuch as ye have done it unto one of the least of these my brethren, ye have done it unto Me."

This war on poverty is not going to be fought in the tradition of emotional crusades. The Economic Opportunities Act of 1964 is a carefully worked-out battle plan based less on praising the Lord than on passing the ammunition. It has been conceived around two central objectives: first, to provide jobs and training, especially for those young people now growing up in poverty and increasingly condemned by lack of economic opportunity to repeat the cycle all over

* Statement before the Ad Hoc Subcommittee on the Poverty Program of the House Education and Labor Committee, March 19, 1964.

again; second, to begin the process of planning and organizing that will bring the entire resources of a community to bear on the specific problem of breaking the cycle of poverty in that community.

Most of the victims of poverty are today the sons and daughters of poverty. Worse than that: of the almost three million children in families receiving public assistance in 1961 under Aid to Dependent Children programs, 40 per cent were descended from grandparents who received this aid. To paraphrase Justice Holmes, three generations of poverty is enough!

In 1962 there were some 11.5 million young persons under the age of eighteen living in families whose total money income was less than $3,000. *Half* these families had incomes below $1,800. Almost two-thirds of the heads of poor families have only eight years or less of schooling. Nearly two out of five of these families are headed by persons who are not listed in the work force at all. The great majority—80 percent—of the poor families in our nation are white. Negroes make up only a fifth of the poor families.

It is a false notion that the poor are concentrated in a few so-called pockets of poverty. They are everywhere in America. If they are out of sight, do not suppose that they are ever more than five miles away.

There is no more desperate plight than that of the poor families headed by women. About a third of the families with women breadwinners in 1962 had incomes under $2,000. About half a million women breadwinners whose husbands were absent were trying to raise school-age children at the same time they supported them.

In April of 1964, there were one million families receiving

assistance through the Aid to Dependent Children program. The average payment to a family was $129 per month last October. This is thirty dollars a week for a family to grow up on. That will keep people alive, but it will not break the cycle of poverty.

It is possible not to face the responsibility of society to provide its children with the health and education and moral instruction that will enable them to become independent, self-sufficient citizens. But it is not possible to escape the penalties of failing to do so. Every undereducated, undertrained youth from a poverty background entering our work force today will cost us approximately $30,000 in various kinds of welfare payments in the course of his life. Either we help the youth or we support the adult. Every dollar we invest now in the youth will save us ten to twenty times that before we are through.

There are some who say that the program tries to go too far too fast, and others who say that it offers too little too slowly. It does recognize that after years of neglect the job must be started on manageable terms and cannot be performed as a miracle. But there is total commitment here; no compromise with principle; and only sensible adjustment to the pace at which principle can be advanced most rapidly.

This program began in 1963 as a result of President Kennedy's growing concern that poverty in America was becoming an inherited trait. The preliminary findings of the Task Force on Manpower Conservation, which showed that one-third of American male youth would be found unqualified for military service, both strengthened this concern and added new urgency to the effort to shape a program. The legislation reflects President Johnson's decision to call poverty by its right, ugly name, and to get down to the business of pulling it out by its roots. It recognizes that these roots are many and diverse, reaching into the fields of health, education, slum surroundings, lack of community facilities and services, lack of motivation and even of hope.

The object is not to make poverty more endurable, but to get rid of it. We are therefore concentrating on jobs, and education and training for work—ways out of poverty. The total antipoverty program includes the tax cut, the Manpower Development and Training Act, the Area Redevelopment Act, and the recently expanded Vocational Education Act. It includes opening up more jobs to those who have been barred from them, through the civil rights program. It includes raising wage levels through the expansion of federal minimum wage coverage, and increasing the distribution of work by making the overtime penalty rates more effective. It must include significant improvements in the unemployment compensation program and the adoption of a program providing medical care for people whose work is done.

The major part of the war on poverty which is covered by the Economic Opportunities Act is that part which involves the training of young people, especially those who have been born into the world of poverty. There is a harsh sentence in the Talmud: that the father who does not teach his son a trade teaches that boy to steal. This is no less true today of the society as a whole.

In June 1963 male youth unemployment reached 21 percent, the highest point since records have been kept. In October 1963 there were 730,000 youths sixteen to twenty-one years old who were out of school, looking for work, and unable to find it. The baby boom is just now rolling into the work force. The number of youths looking for jobs is now rising, and will shortly begin to soar. But so far the supply of jobs for young people has not been increasing. During 1963 the number of jobs for young workers in America was not increased by a single job. Every added member of the teen-age work force resulted in one additional unemployed teen-ager. Although unemployment declined in May 1964 to the lowest point in four years, about one out of six teen-agers in our labor force could not find a job.

The Economic Opportunities Act of 1964 contains provision for the assistance, through work and training programs, of between 300,000 and 400,000 boys and girls every year. The Job Corps program provided for by Title I-A of the act will provide training and work camp experience for young men and women who need most of all to be given a new environment in which to develop their talents. A second part of this youth training and work program, which will be administered through the Department of Labor, is provided for in Title I-B. It contemplates the development of work-training programs, in Neighborhood Youth Corps, for 200,000 boys and girls the first year. The Job-Study program set up by Title I-C of the act will permit boys and girls who might otherwise have to drop out of school for economic reasons to meet their needs.

The Economic Opportunities Act of 1964 provides an arsenal of weapons from which to choose in mounting the attack on the various problems of youth, poverty, and unemployment. The infection of poverty undermines the national strength in many different ways, and only a unified counterattack will bring the victory we seek as a nation.

Fighting poverty means fighting the cumulative and interrelated effect of every aspect of it.

To do less will be to lose.

This act promises no miracles, pretends to no panacea. It is, though, the product of a hard-headed idealism which is the truest expression of the American character. It offers a sound beginning, a careful plan, an attainable goal, a practical dedication of the nation to the purpose of the great society. It affirms our purpose as a nation, to live by the same moral code we profess as individuals.

Poverty in the Cities*

Speaking at the University of Michigan commencement ceremonies in May, President Lyndon B. Johnson described the "places where we can begin to build the great society." The first of these, he said, must be our cities. Noting that in the next fifty years the population of the cities will double and that there will be required new facilities "equal to all those built since this country was settled," President Johnson called for a rebuilding of the entire urban United States "to make the American city a place where future generations will come, not only to live, but to live the good life."

We must not underestimate the dimension of this project. The extent to which so many cities have been permitted to become ugly, decrepit and inhospitable places was not intended or even realized. We knew the scandal of the heedless and wasteful misuse of our natural resources during the nineteenth century, the pillaging of forests and rivers and soil. Yet we have failed to sense the equal scandal of the twentieth-century ravaging of the American city. Too often it was developed only to meet the immediate demands of an industry or a commerce which then moved on. Its housing was designed to yield a profit from the payment of poverty rents.

* 1964 Annual Conference of Mayors, New York, New York, May 25, 1964.

Then it was knocked apart by automobiles and trucks. Abandoned by its middle classes, it became a final resting place for the poor of America.

If these statements are too broad, our cities nevertheless reflect the central fact of the contemporary culture: that it is one of incomparable well-being in general, but with increasingly serious concentrations of want and deprivation. The slums one comes upon suddenly, just off streets of spacious homes, are the physical manifestations of a prosperity pock-marked by patches and pockets of poverty. So it is that President Johnson's call for the rebuilding of America's cities is closely linked to the attack now being mounted against poverty in America. Slums do not result from the rotting of the materials used to build their walls and streets, but from the rotting of the lives of the people who live there. Buildings are not condemned until after they have been lived in by condemned people. There will be lasting urban renewal only as there is developed first an adequate program of human renewal.

Where, then, do we start on such a program?

This choice may be made for us, as part of a developing situation we are inclined to view in different terms.

In most of the cities of the nation there is today a wavering between new confidence and new concern. A strong and thriving economy is going month by month from record to record. There is unprecedented agreement on major issues of public policy among a majority of American voters, and of those in effective control of the Congress and the Executive Branch. It is nonetheless generally expected that the months ahead will be troubled, turbulent, perhaps even dangerous.

The occasion of this mixture of high hopes and deep anxieties is, of course, the civil rights movement. The great question about the civil rights movement has been too little asked. This question is not whether this movement will continue. It will. Neither is there any question whether it will prevail in most of the essential demands now being made. It will, as it must. The great question is what institutional form the civil rights movement will assume on a permanent basis. And the answer to this question depends on the nation's response to this movement.

It is possible that what will develop here is another well-organized, disciplined, special-interest group representing one particular segment of the population. We are entitled to a higher hope: that the current civil rights movement will become a broadly based, integrated, and creative force for the advancement of human rights and the improvement of the human condition throughout the United States, and for the rebuilding of America's cities.

Nothing could more profoundly underestimate the leaders and the rank and file of this movement, nor more seriously misjudge the nature of the conditions which they protest, and which they have undertaken to change, than to assume that they are concerned exclusively or even primarily with such matters as formal segregation or overt, calculated discrimination. To the contrary, the civil rights movement in instance after instance has shown itself to be profoundly concerned with the entire complex of economic, and cultural, and sociological forces which are precisely those forces that have turned the American city into slums: the forces of poverty, unemployment, ignorance, and alienation. The civil rights movement has developed as a massive, militant force demanding that something be done, not just about racial discrimination, but about conditions which include the worst of urban life in America.

It will be required first, to meet these demands, that there be full recognition of how serious the situation has become. We are familiar with the national employment and unemployment statistics; but we are not at all clear about what the underuse of men and women has meant in human terms and how deeply the infection of unemployment has set in among the poor in America, especially among the minority groups.

There can be no mistaking the relation between rising unemployment and rising welfare dependency. It is a familiar enough matter to express alarm and dismay over the ever-mounting number of recipients under the Aid to Dependent Children program, now nearing four million persons. The number seems to go up and up. Yet in actual fact there have been nine years since the program began in 1936 when the number of recipients has declined. These were the years of the Second World War and the Korean War, the only periods in modern times when the American poor have been employed.

The real reason for the resurgence of the civil rights movement in the recent past has been the growing awareness among Negroes of what rising unemployment has been doing to the Negro family structure. In 1949, for example, 9 percent of white families in America were headed by a female. Thirteen years later, in 1962, the proportion was still 9 percent. Among Negroes, the proportion during this period rose from 19 percent to 23 percent. There are figures which show, from year to year, the number of families with both the husband and wife living, but with the husband absent. In 1947 the percent of "White Married Families with the Husband Absent" was 4.1 percent. By 1962 it had moved up hardly at all, to 4.4 percent. In the same period, the percent of "Negro Married Families with the Husband Absent" rose from 13.7 percent to 20.5 percent.

There is unmistakable correlation between the rate of male Negro unemployment and the proportion of "Negro Married Families" in which the husband is absent. The long rise in the "Absent Husbands" series is accompanied by an even sharper rise in figures for "Unemployment—Males." The relation can also be charted from year to year. For example, in 1954 Negro male unemployment jumped from 4.4 percent for the previous year to 9.2 percent. The year after that, 1955, the proportion of married families with absent husbands went up sharply to 21.9 percent. Next, unemployment declined, and one year later the "Absent Husbands" figure went down. In the recession of 1958, Negro male unemployment jumped from 8.4 percent to 13.7 percent, and the next year the "Absent Husbands" figure rose sharply again, from 19.8 percent to 23.3 percent, the all-time high. Since then, as unemployment has moderated slightly, so has the rate of absent husbands, always trailing the unemployment figures by a year.

These figures only illustrate the close interrelationship between the problems of civil rights and of poverty. Of all Negro families, half are listed among the poor. So long as civil rights issues are mixed with the desperate insecurities of communities brutalized by bad housing and poor education, and harassed by unemployment, we can expect little in the way of social peace in the American cities or the countryside.

The essence of the President's civil rights program is to settle for once and all the guarantee of equal opportunity for all Americans. The essence of the President's War on Poverty is to ensure that every American has an opportunity to be equal.

VI

FULL EMPLOYMENT: AUTOMATION AND A MANPOWER PROGRAM

MILLIONS OF PEOPLE in this country are today seriously concerned about whether there is going to be enough work to go around. This is a false fear. We may or may not prove willing and able to make the decisions necessary to maintain full employment. I think we will. But if we fail to achieve full employment, it will be for lack of courage and common sense, not for lack of work to be done.

It is this simple: the things to be done—meeting consumer needs and desires which are today unsatisfied, cleaning out the slums and building the schools and hospitals and roads and water supply and transit and recreational facilities we need, moving back into the export position we once held, making contact with the rest of the universe—will require all the men and women who are available *and trained* to work. Automation, the fullest possible degree of technological development, will be essential to doing this job.

It is a dangerous misconception that attaining full employment is a matter of people winning a race against computers for a limited and fixed number of jobs. That race would be lost by people. Trying to "protect" present jobs, through either private or public efforts, will be completely ineffectual.

The only worse error would be to assume that there is some kind of unseen hand in the economy which is guiding all that we call "automation" so that it will work out automatically to the advantage of everyone concerned. There isn't such a hand. What is required is, first, the action necessary to stimulate the markets and uses for people's production and service; second, those adjustments required to see to it that the human price of automation is spread as widely as the human profit from automation; and third, the revolution in education which is required if people are to develop the skills and knowledge the scientific society demands.

We have already met a series of challenges in a manner which reflects a developing commitment to a bold policy for achieving full employment:

(1) Faced, in 1961, with the issue of whether the nation should be alerted to the unemployment problem or permitted to ignore it for fear of upsetting "business confidence," President Kennedy expressed the national conscience when he said that he had "no intention of learning to live with prolonged and severe unemployment, with all that it means in human misery and economic waste." Congress responded by passing the Area Redevelopment Act, the Temporary Extended Unemployment Compensation Act, and the Manpower Development and Training Act.

(2) Automation has given new and urgent meaning to the age-old problem of new machinery displacing workers. Some have suggested that we can no longer afford to permit unlimited technological change because of our high unemploy-

ment and the vast possibilities for displacement suggested by the merger of the computer and the machine. The consensus in all segments of the economy is, however, that automation is not only inevitable but necessary if we are to remain competitive and to secure the better life which the automated economy offers. The message has been clearly passed, in public statements and in revisions of the tax depreciation schedules, that investment in new technology is encouraged.

(3) Concern about high unemployment has also prompted proposals that employment could best be increased by a statutory reduction in the work week, or by reducing the minimum wage, or by restricting imports. The general decision has been not to move in these directions. Proposals to cut the work week by legislative action have been rejected. Amendments to the Fair Labor Standards Act were enacted in 1961 raising the minimum wage and extending its coverage. The Trade Expansion Act of 1962 manifests the national confidence in freer trade and adjustment assistance, and not in higher tariffs.

(4) Despite significant progress toward increasing economic growth and reducing unemployment, it was apparent by late 1962 that further action was needed if we were to attain the goal of economic prosperity and full employment. The action generally considered most needed was a reduction in taxes to stimulate private investment and consumption. The great majority of all Americans insisted that we could afford and needed to invest this much in our own system. Their support produced the 1964 tax cut.

(5) Given the pressure on the dollar budget resulting from the need to provide an adequate defense and an effective program of foreign aid, it would have been easy to decide

that we could not afford additional spending for education, public housing, public works or mass transit facilities. The various education bills which have been adopted, the Housing Act of 1961, the Accelerated Public Works Act of 1962, and the Mass Transit Act of 1964 reflect the nation's contrary decision.

An impressive start has been made, but additional action will be required to produce an adequate and comprehensive manpower program. Such a program will give full recognition both to the demands of industry and to the needs of individuals. There is need for improved communication among educators, businessmen and employment service officials concerning training and the identification of prospective job vacancies. There must be a national undertaking to achieve full utilization of the talents and potential of all Americans.

Balancing the Manpower Budget*

The United States adopted, in the Employment Act of 1946, a national policy of maintaining full employment. This was an event of significance and was so regarded at the time, but it was an event of limited consequence. A policy was adopted without a program for carrying it out. The result was not full employment but rather a series of ups and downs; none of them, fortunately, drastic, but nonetheless leading to the period since 1957 during every month of which, saving only February 1960, unemployment has been 5 percent or more.

This might appear to mark the bankruptcy of the 1946 policy. Five percent unemployment in the United States means at least four million men and women out of work, with all that this implies in terms of human want, humiliation, and loss of purpose. It means an annual tax on the economy of between three and four billion dollars for unemployment benefits. It means the irretrievable loss, the waste, of eight million man-hours of production every year.

This 5 percent U.S. unemployment compares with percentages of 1 to 3 percent in France, West Germany, Italy, Japan, and Sweden. In 1960 the seven largest foreign industrial nations of the free world had a combined labor force

* Midwestern Governors Conference, Chicago, Illinois, December 13, 1962; White House Regional Conference, Chicago, Illinois, November 7, 1961.

of 143 million, more than twice that of the United States; yet their total combined unemployment was three million, or 25 percent, less than ours.

We are not in the habit of running last in such competitions.

Yet to paint the picture this way is to distort it. It was Cardinal Richelieu's wry observation that he could, with six sentences selected from the writings of any man, hang him. It is possible today, with the data at hand, to prove with selected statistics either the success or failure, the health or debility, the vigor or apathy, of almost any large economic institution. No statistics must be permitted to cloud the fact that the economy of the United States is a success beyond parallel in history; that it has produced a standard of living for most of its members which is the envy, and now the goal, of all the world's people; that this country defines poverty now by income levels rather than in terms of starvation and death in the streets; and that most of the unemployed here can better satisfy more of life's needs than the majority of those who work from dawn to dark in much of the world.

The point, though, is that we measure what we are by what we could be and what we propose to be. Every individual person in this country who wants a job and is denied it represents a proper and unsatisfied claim against democracy's pledge of equal opportunity for all. Capitalism will have lost its conscience, and America her title deed, if there is any compromise with the idea of full economic opportunity in this country for everybody willing to work. We reject any proposition that a nation able to put itself to all-out production for war can become so muscle-bound that it cannot do the same thing in times of peace.

The fact is, furthermore, that we are developing now the full employment program which the 1946 policy declaration lacked.

Such a program begins with a willingness to face the truth about unemployment. This means not ignoring joblessness in order to protect business confidence or compromising with it because of fear about inflation. It means recognizing that four million unemployed is a deficit as deplorable as one measured in dollars, and that balancing the manpower budget at full employment is a matter of top priority importance.

There are three necessary action fronts.

First, there must be adequate assistance to the jobless and those who are at the bottom of the economic ladder. The Temporary Extended Unemployment Compensation Act of 1961 and the increase and extension of the statutory minimum wage provide new safeguards against distress. So does the crew leader registration law, a first step toward meeting the tragic plight of the 500,000 migratory farm workers and their families, pathetic derelicts of the economy. The basic unemployment insurance system must also be improved, the amount and duration of benefits permanently increased, the coverage broadened, and uniform standards established.

But unemployment insurance benefits are only economic aspirin tablets. They dull the pain, but they don't cure unemployment.

A second requirement is a large-scale training and retraining program. Unemployment meant, in 1935 and in 1946, the temporary interruption of a man's performance of a job to which he was expected to return. Unemployment means today, in many cases, a complete disruption of an employment relationship; so that a man's eventual return to work may well be with a different employer, very possibly at a job requiring entirely different skills. The new jobs, furthermore, will not all be in the areas where the manpower for them is available, for our economy is also shifting geographically. One out of every six jobs today is in California, Texas, or Florida. In 1951 only one in nine jobs was in those states. The problems of necessarily increased worker mobility must also be faced squarely.

Part of this training and relocation assistance can be supplied privately, and some companies and unions are working out imaginative programs to meet these needs. But too often the situation will be what it is for several hundred employees in an Ohio plant who recently received five-day notice that the plant was being shut down. "You can be assured," the company wrote them, "that our representatives will be available to help you in obtaining State unemployment compensation and also to help you in your efforts to find suitable employment with other employers." That's all. It is a fair assumption that more consideration was given, in the shutting down of that plant, to the machinery which was in it than to the men and women who worked it.

Only a flexible, maneuverable, adaptable labor force will be capable of meeting the force of change. The training and relocation provisions of the Area Redevelopment Act, the Manpower Development and Training Act, and the Trade Expansion Act are directed toward this goal.

Yet training and relocation programs, vital as they are, have meaning only to the extent that there are jobs to be filled. The ultimate answer to unemployment is not insurance. It is not retraining. It is more jobs.

If there are key statistics in this situation, they are these two: first, that an average of over two million new workers will be entering the work force each year during this decade, which is 50 percent more than during the fifties; second, that a comparison of employment and production figures indicates that machines are now taking up each week the equivalent of 35,000 jobs, which means 1,820,000 jobs a year.

To realize the magnitude of these facts is to recognize the puniness, the self-defeating quality, of any thinking about unemployment in terms of protecting present jobs—by make-work practices, by protectionist tariff policies, or by fighting automation. These are short cuts across economic quicksand.

There is no short cut to full employment. The additional millions of new jobs which will be needed every year can only come from expanding the economy, from opening up new markets, from doing what is necessary to put unused American capital and manpower at work to fill unmet American needs, from building the New America whose blueprints we already have before us.

The fact that we have not been growing fast enough should not obscure the clear promise that we can do what needs to be done. We have the resources and the skills to make the greatest economic advance in our history. America is like Gulliver in Lilliput—a giant, held down by a mass of small doubts and restrictions, needing only to exert the strength of its convictions to realize its full potential. The hard truth of the matter is that nothing—nothing!—is needed to put this country on a full employment basis except the decision to do it.

This decision will not be made by prisoners of hope or captives of hidebound conservatism. It will not come from leadership with a bedside manner, telling people only what they would like to hear. It will be made only by a fully informed people determined to do the things we need to do, the things we want to do, and the things we can do to prove that unemployment is not a price of the free, capitalistic society.

We need, for example, and agree that we need, 140,000 new schoolrooms in this country. It would take about one billion man-hours of labor to build those 140,000 classrooms. Yet we are wasting this year, through unemployment, eight times that many man-hours of productive labor. It is an interesting coincidence that the cost of those schoolrooms would be approximately four billion dollars, which is also the amount of unemployment and relief benefits we are paying out this year—for work not performed because it wasn't available!

The matching of our need for schools and part of our unused manpower is only one illustration of the "paradox," in President Kennedy's phrase, "of idleness coexisting with unfilled national needs"—needs for hospitals, homes, roads, parks, water supply systems, and, most significantly of all, limitless unmet private consumer demands.

If there were war, America would agree immediately on an unlimited step-up in production, and would get that production. There would be more jobs than could be filled. If we will agree in the same way to step up production for a better America at peace, the same results will follow.

No economy in history has had greater opportunity to show what is the quality of its living once the terrible, grinding anxiety for daily bread is removed from all its citizens. The only question is whether we will use what we have. It is the question of the parable of the talents: whether we will choose to bury our talents or to use them. There can be only one answer: that we will implement the policy of full employment, and redeem our pledge of opportunity for all.

Automation and Education*

"Does automation," the question is repeatedly put, "create more jobs than it destroys?"

Like so many questions that are hard to answer, part of the difficulty with this one is that it isn't nearly so good a question as it seems to be. "Automation" may or may not be (I think it is) anything more than the present stage of a process that began with the first use of the hammer, the lever, the inclined plane, and the wheel. What is more serious, the question invites and appears to warrant a short answer, so that a deliberative response will appear either uninformed or equivocal; and the truest short answer available will only conceal the real importance of what is involved—as though the New York *Sun* had given Virginia a short "no" about Santa Claus.

That short answer here would have to be that automation—machines, technological invention, or what you will—is (a) inevitable; and (b) essential to the necessary growth of the economy. It need only be considered what would happen if all invention were to stop.

This hasn't always been clear. It is not long ago that one of

* National Committee for the Support of Public Schools, Washington, D.C., April 9, 1963; Sidney Hillman Lecture, University of Rochester, Rochester, New York, April 3, 1963.

the European governments prohibited the use of typewriters in public offices so as to avoid putting pen wielders out of work. Here in the United States, in the 1930's, there was a Congressional investigation into whether, at that time of high unemployment, a policy should be adopted of slowing up the kind of developments we now call "automation." That was only a few years before America was being pushed to the ultimate of its capacity in order to meet the demands which alien forces pressed upon the free world.

Yet, easy as it is to laugh at the mistakes of the past, we usually do so while we are repeating them, and a serious problem arises today from the attempts in some quarters to fight against machines and "automation." Automation means employment, not unemployment. The only way we can possibly maintain a standard of living higher than that of any other country in a world that is becoming smaller and more competitive with each passing year is by doing the most efficient job that can conceivably be done.

In some people's thinking, this is all there is to be said about automation. There is a selective interpretation of history which develops around a concept of progress measured in terms of automobile horsepower and tail fins and the growth in the Gross National Product. It is part of this interpretation of history that you can't stop progress, which is probably true; and the corollary is often suggested that you can't help progress or humanize it, which does not follow from the first proposition and is probably not true at all. But I haven't heard for a long time the phrase so common in the decade of the twenties, about "the inevitability of progress."

The other side of the question about the effect of automation on jobs, and therefore on people, is that in terms of *particular individuals* the casualty lists are beginning to mount to alarming proportions. For the new job or jobs a new machine creates may be hundreds of miles from the one it destroyed, in a different industry, requiring a different skill, and of no value whatsoever to the displaced person. Only if there were an infinitely tighter manpower situation throughout the country than in fact exists, only if labor were far more mobile than in fact it is, and only if there were in the work force a much larger degree of skill and transferability of skills than in fact there is—only if all these assumptions were made, contrary to fact, would the aggregative question of whether automation means more or fewer jobs cover the real question which is involved.

The beneficiaries of automation are, for the most part, that large and fortunate American majority who are fairly well educated, skilled, comfortable financially, and probably white. Its victims are in the main the less educated, the poor, often nonwhite.

There is the distinct possibility that technology's rapid advance will exacerbate the "minority group" problem just at the point where our laws and practices affecting it have finally caught up with our conscience. And it now appears likely that the most severe impact of automation will be on the boys and girls who are now entering the work force in unprecedented numbers, a great many of them lacking the education and training to compete with machines.

Indeed, the broader problem can be best suggested in terms of the Case of the Computer Versus the Dropout.

No problem in the country has been less clearly seen than what has come to be called the "dropout problem." It would be more accurate, in the first place, to call them "pushouts" for the fault is rarely theirs as much as ours. But the more important error in the general thinking about it lies in the fallacious popular assumption that the dropout problem is one of an increasing number of boys and girls leaving school prematurely. To the contrary; each year for the last twenty-five or thirty-five years the number of dropouts has gone down. In 1960 the percentage of dropouts was only half what it had been in 1925. As of 1953, for every 1,000 students who had earlier gone into the fifth grade, 504 finished high school. By 1960, this figure had gone up to about 605. By 1962, it was up to about 640.

The dropout problem is not that more are dropping out. It is that there is significantly less demand for unskilled workers in the work force today than there was before. The unskilled jobs left are being taken by older people who themselves are displaced by machines and are bumped down into the unskilled reservoir at the bottom.

Thirty years ago, I was teaching *Macbeth* and *Hamlet* and the idiosyncrasies of the split infinitive to a group of high school students in a Midwest industrial community. I remember the pressure of the constant realization that very little of it was getting through to very many of them. But it didn't matter. That was in a town where most of the boys were going into the boiler works, and if the girls didn't get married, they would probably get work at the glove factory. Most of those jobs were unskilled. So it was just as well to expose them all to syntax and Shakespeare, as a kind of by-product to the preparation of a few of their colleagues for college.

Today, however, boys and girls simply have to be trained

to fit into an economy which no longer includes the unskilled work they could get before. Anybody who drops out of school may very well be committing economic suicide. Automation demands that the educational system assume the responsibility of seeing to it that nobody leaves school until he or she is prepared to do the kind of work that is now available.

The failure to discharge this responsibility is reflected in the degree to which the burden of unemployment is falling now upon younger people. It has been a mistake to talk about unemployment in terms of its affecting 5 or 6 percent of the total labor force in this country. It is that only in the aggregate. I think of Walter Heller's identification of the law of averages as being the means by which to prove that if someone is standing with one foot in the refrigerator and one foot on the stove, he is on the average comfortable.

In 1953 the unemployment rate for the fourteen-to-nineteen-year-olds was about 6 percent. Now, ten years later, it is 12 percent! It has increased for the nonwhite teen-ager from about 6 percent in 1953 to about 21 percent in 1963; and for the nonwhite younger female group it is now almost 30 percent.

There are now about 3,500,000 boys and girls between the ages of fourteen and nineteen who are out of school and "in the work force," either working or looking for work they cannot find. About 2,700,000 have jobs, although many of them have too little training to feel any security about the future. The other 800,000 are in the out-of-school, out-of-work group. They make up a fifth of all the unemployed in the country. Most of them are unprepared for the kind of jobs which are now available.

There is another, more disturbing group whose size can only be estimated. They are not counted among the unemployed because they have given up even looking for work. (The unemployment statistics include only those who are "actively looking for work.") The best estimates put about 500,000 boys and girls in this lost battalion today, with the number increasing at a frightening rate. Statistics tell this story poorly. It is clearer in my thinking in terms of two conversations. One was with a young girl, probably seventeen or eighteen years old, standing outside a dilapidated home in a small town in eastern Kentucky. I asked her whether she was in school, and she shook her head silently. Then I asked whether she was working. She said she was not. When I went on to ask whether she was looking for work, she stood there quietly for a moment and then answered with her own question: "Where?"

A few weeks later I had a similar conversation with a boy, of about the same age, on a street corner in Harlem. His answers were like the girl's, except that when I asked whether he was looking for work his reply was "Why?"

Those two youngsters don't know it, but they and the hundreds of thousands like them are the price we are paying today for the "progress" we call automation. Yes, there will be more jobs with automation than there would be without it. That has to be true. The real question, though, is how many people are going to be left out. And the answer to that question is, bluntly: almost all who are not educated. The machines have, in general, the equivalent of a high school education, and they work for less than a living wage.

So I see the nub of the automation question not in terms of whether there will be more jobs or fewer, but in terms of what must be done to prepare *everyone* for the kind of jobs there will be in a work force where machines do the unskilled work.

This means a virtual revolution in our thinking about education.

We have been supplying twelve years of free education, and requiring, in most states, that children start school when they are six and stay in school until they are sixteen. The majority, who are not going on to college, are given the training which is needed as preparation for the minority, those whose parents can afford sending them to college.

If this made sense a century ago, when most of these educational principles were adopted, it doesn't now.

What is most obvious is that there must be a substantial expansion of a vocational education program which will equip for the jobs that exist those who will not have the chance to go on to college.

There should be serious consideration given to adding two more years of free education for those who need it and will use it—not just two more years of the same kind of thing which has been offered traditionally, but whatever it is that is required to meet the present situation. And it should be required, in one form or another, that a person stay in school until he is prepared to carry himself in the society.

There will have to be sober appraisal, too, of the question of whether, especially in areas of serious underprivilege, children should not start school at an earlier age than we have been considering necessary and advisable. There is increasing reason to believe that it is between the ages of perhaps three and six that there is the most serious crippling of motivation among the children of poverty and underprivilege.

There must also be better opportunities for education at the higher end of the scale. With more and more of the good jobs requiring college training, some way must be found to make college available to qualified youngsters in low-income families. A recent study shows that if you line up a typical high school class by their parents' income alone, not by their own academic standing, 46 percent of the students in the top third will go to college, and only 13 percent of the graduates in the poorest third will get to college. This is not fair, it's not the American way, and it's not good for America.

Some of the suggested changes in the educational system obviously have a substantial price tag on them. More education will be expensive. A training program will be expensive. A Youth Employment Act will be expensive. Yet the price tag on the proposed Youth Employment Act of 1963, which would provide for the training of sixty to sixty-five thousand children a year, comes to what we spend on national defense every sixteen hours! This comparison in no way suggests that there is unnecessary spending on national defense. There isn't. This simply identifies, in comparative terms, the cost involved in the programs needed to educate our children.

Yet, if the costs were infinitely more than that, the fact would remain that every single dollar spent to educate or train a worker, particularly a young worker, will be returned many times over. The alternative is to carry people the rest of their lives, at a high price in terms of public aid, unemployment insurance benefits, institutional costs, the contribution of family and friends and private organizations—a price infinitely larger than the cost of training them now to make them productive members of the society. Such training would make them not only good, productive members of the society, but good customers, too; and, equally significantly in connection with the point of costs, it would also make taxpayers out of them.

There is talk about not passing debts on to the next generation. The worst possible debt that could be passed on to the next generation would be if its members were not trained to make a living. This is not somebody else's debt; it is a debt of this generation, and it is one that must be paid.

To return, then, to the question of whether automation creates or destroys more jobs, there are these parts to the answer: first, that technological development is an essential element in the expanding economy and that in this sense it contributes to the making of the increased number of jobs which a steadily and rapidly growing labor force demands; second, that this process undeniably results in the taking of jobs from some people and the denial of jobs to others, resulting in the creation of an exceedingly serious situation because this loss is suffered by those least equipped to cope with the situation.

There is Karel Capek's play of the early twenties, *R. U. R.* —"Rossum's Universal Robots." It is the story of how the scientists develop their robots to higher and higher degrees of perfection, until finally the robots learn how to make other robots. At the end of the third act, the curtains at the sides and the back of the stage part, the robots come marching in, form in solid phalanxes, turn toward the audience, and come plodding stolidly out—at people. Just as they reach the footlights the lights go out and the play is over.

That is fiction, drama, a poet's warning. But the ending is false. Robots—machines—automation—technology—science! Either these are men's tools, or men are the tools of tools, depending solely upon whether we choose to qualify our sons and daughters to use the forces we have unlocked. The economic alternative to automation would be stagnation. The answer to whatever human problems it poses is education.

Economics and People*

I approach the subject of fiscal and monetary policy partly in awe, and partly with the thought in mind of Will Rogers' proposal for stopping the German submarine menace in World War I. "All we need to do," he said, "is heat the Atlantic Ocean up to 212 degrees Fahrenheit. Then the subs will have to come to the surface and we can pick them off one by one. I know," he went on, "that somebody is going to want to know how to warm up that much water. But I can't worry about that. It's a matter of detail and I am a policymaker."

To suggest the inherent limitations of "policy" conclusions, particularly in a society where decision-making depends upon common consent, is perhaps to risk the appearance of naïveté, or even anti-intellectualism. Surely it would be the worst absurdity to think about attempting to govern a nation of 190 million people without taking full advantage of all available navigational guides. It seems appropriate, nevertheless, to note the shortcomings and even the dangers of too great reliance, in the guiding of government, on the shooting of the economic stars.

There is probably little real danger that the lay decision-makers in a free society will ever become the slaves of a

* Conference on Fiscal and Monetary Policy, President's Advisory Committee on Labor-Management Policy, Washington, D.C., November 15, 1962.

cosmic inductivity which escalates particulars into a vast, and deceptive, universality. Proper consideration will be given to expert testimony that such and such a fiscal and monetary policy will produce a growth rate of X percent, resulting in a Gross National Product of Y billions of dollars, accompanied by an unemployment rate of no more than Z percent; whereupon the problem of poverty will go away. But there will be a healthy skepticism, at the same time, of the statistical wonders that emerge from the world of macro-economists, and a healthy realization that the meshes of their nets are so wide that a fantastic number of human beings can slip through without the statistics ever showing it.

It is becoming increasingly apparent that the American economy is capable of going from strength to greater strength with only marginal, if any, improvements in the lives of the one out of five American families which in 1960 earned annual incomes of less than $3,000. This means, since our basic purpose is the enrichment of all people's lives, that we will have to check the results of any aggregative equations against whatever we know of more specific situations.

The fact of four million unemployed people in this country is so deplorable a situation, in human terms, as to warrant indignant intolerance of any explanation which is advanced for it in terms of any kind of economic analysis. If the answer to a suggestion to advance the purpose of full employment is that it will contribute to inflation, an unbalanced budget, or an unfavorable dollar balance, that cannot be the end of it; for full employment is itself an ultimate purpose. And surely the meaning of full employment cannot be arrived at by working back from an assumption about the minimum degree of unemployment which can be achieved without threat of inflation. It would be a serious error if the country were to become conditioned to the idea that 4 percent is, for any reason, a satisfactory unemployment rate.

There must be no misunderstanding: inflation, fiscal irresponsibility, and international bankruptcy are vices the economy simply cannot afford. But neither can it afford unemployment. The point is that in an economy characterized by vast unmet needs, and limitless resources in materials, men, and ideas, there is no need to choose between these evils. We are entitled to insist upon both growth and stability, and that we not deny ourselves the necessary growth because of fears that we can't take it if we get it.

It is relevant that there is a tendency to suggest that whatever can be brought within a single phrase, or a single statistic, is a single problem—"unemployment" for example, especially 5.X percent unemployment, seasonally adjusted. This has the effect of submerging the human implications of problems, by encouraging misleading short answers to deceptively short questions.

It is asked: What is *the* solution to unemployment? To economic stagnation? To inflation? What is the answer to the dollar deficit? To Cuba? Or to Berlin? Or to Communism? Such questions invite answers that are short, concise—and wrong; and there are charlatans aplenty to use these easy answers to drive hard answers out of the market. A society that relies increasingly, furthermore, on machines which can produce only arithmetic answers will need to be on guard against limiting its questions to those for which the machines can produce replies.

The monthly announcement by the Labor Department's

Bureau of Labor Statistics of a "seasonally adjusted" decimal-point unemployment percentage figure contributes to the illusion of a single unemployment problem when in fact there are a dozen significantly different unemployment situations. Some of those reported as unemployed in any given month are the sole support of families; others are youngsters who have dropped out of school. Some are men and women moving from one job to another with a comparatively short interval in between; others have been out of work over six months; still others are workers in seasonal industries who routinely support themselves by unemployment insurance during their off season. Some are skilled workers in basically prosperous labor markets who are waiting for plants to be retooled or for the weather to improve; others are unskilled workers in areas doomed to indefinite economic distress. Some are out of work because machines have taken their place. Others are victims of racial discrimination.

This series is of incalculable value for broad comparative purpose. Each monthly figure serves, however, only the purpose of the reading on a thermometer used to take a temperature. If it shows a fever, it does nothing to reveal the cause of it or what to do about it.

The worst difficulty in meeting the unemployment problem is not a lack of policies regarding it, but the lack of real national comprehension and understanding of it. The hardest part of doing anything about the 5 percent who are unemployed is the 95 percent who are employed. When we report that the answer to the unemployment problem lies in an expansion of the Gross National Product by 4 or 4.5 percent a year, this doesn't mean much to very many people. And when it is added that this requires an increase in the

Gross National Product of twenty-five to thirty billion dollars a year, there is the additional reaction of impotence on the part of the individual in the presence of a problem of this magnitude. Responsible discussions of policy-making must take account of the necessity of implementing the right answers through the processes of a free, decision-making society.

The decision to reduce taxes, to incur deliberately a temporarily increased budgetary imbalance as a means of invigorating the economy and stimulating the use of idle plant and manpower capacity, is a decision of unprecedented boldness. The national reaction to it is encouraging evidence of a broader potential for popular understanding of involved economic considerations than a lot of people had assumed.

It is reasonable to expect the same kind of developing understanding of the parallel need for an enlightened manpower policy, to meet the needs of the economy as it gets into step with its potential. Without such a policy there would be the danger of finding ourselves with a work force too untrained and too immobile to meet the new demands that will be pressed upon it.

A vigorous, expanding economy involves a very high rate of change in manpower demands. New factories and offices open as old ones close; new products are introduced as others disappear; some industries and areas become more active as others slow up. There is the possibility of hardship and waste here unless measures designed to encourage such developments are accompanied by equally vigorous efforts to provide new skills and find new jobs for workers who are affected by the changes.

The Area Redevelopment Act, the Manpower Development and Training Act, and the Accelerated Public Works Act mark great advances along this line. So does the program established by President Kennedy and developed so vigorously by Vice President Johnson to eliminate, through the work of the Committee on Equal Employment Opportunity, racial discrimination in employment by the government and by government contractors.

A great deal more remains to be done in the specific treatment of specific problems. This is hard, grubby, unglamorous work. It involves looking into the special facts of particular cases, and molding programs to meet specific needs. It requires the realization that big as we have become as a nation we remain a people whose essential pride is our recognition of the individuality of human beings.

It may very well be that the ultimate goals which make sense are best identified in terms of meeting the needs we know we have and know we can meet: more education, better health services, improved transportation, new recreational facilities, and a higher standard of living. If we met our needs in these areas, there would be full employment and adequate economic growth.

Perhaps primary importance should be attached to general re-education in the real meaning of the national budget. At some point it will have to be made clearer than it has been so far that certain types of public expenditures are for investment which will yield returns in the size of the economy and in future savings.

Wise and imaginative development of fiscal and monetary policy is essential to keep the economy strong and free enough to achieve its potential. So is the development of a more enlightened manpower policy. The complete answer to the debate between those who attribute unemployment to inadequate demand and those who emphasize its structural aspects is that both problems are present, and both must be met. It is as important in the one area as the other to take full account of the essentially human equation which it is the society's central purpose to solve.

Freer Trade and Fuller Employment*

The Trade Expansion Act of 1962 provided a testing and a vindication of the democratic process. As a rule we are more sensitive and responsive, politically, to the outcries of those who may be hurt than to the interests of those who will be helped. But in the Trade Act the Congress, recognizing the need for boldness and for confidence in our system, gave the President a broad grant of authority to reduce tariffs. At the same time, as proposed by the Administration, provisions were also made for adjustment assistance to firms and workers adversely affected by imports and for international agreements to deal with situations of market disruption in industries which might be seriously affected by sharp increases in imports.

The Trade Expansion Act, however, is only a policy and a grant of authority. It will not, by itself, expand exports one dollar. Nor will the reciprocal trade agreements executed under its authority. Such expansion must be accomplished by American business with the cooperation and encouragement of American labor.

It will help stimulate this expansion if there is clear reali-

---

* White House Conference on Export Expansion, Washington, D.C., September 17, 1963; Testimony before the Subcommittee on Foreign Economic Policy of the Joint Economic Committee, December 13, 1961.

zation of the importance of freer trade in the national effort to achieve fuller employment.

Every increase of one billion dollars of exports means an increase of about 150,000 jobs.

The best available estimates are that at least 1,200,000 American workers owe their jobs to the direct production of goods and commodities for export. Another 1,450,000 workers are employed in producing the materials which go into those export products (such as steel and aluminum, fertilizer and plastics), in generating the power to produce them, in providing transportation for them, and so forth. Every job of this kind also means the creation of the equivalent of one additional job to fill the consumer needs of the worker involved and those dependent on him. This means, in round numbers, that the employment of approximately five million American workers is today dependent, directly and indirectly, on this country's export trade.

Of the estimated total of 2,650,000 workers who owe their employment most directly to exports, some 1,850,000 are engaged in the production of nonagricultural products and services; the other 800,000 are engaged in agriculture. One out of every five workers in the machine tool industry is employed because of exports. The agricultural produce from one out of every six acres is sold abroad. Forty percent of the value of domestic production of civilian aircraft is exported.

In 1953 the United States' exports of manufactured goods amounted to 36 percent of the total exports of the ten leading nations (which accounted for 85 percent of the world's total). Our share of this market has dropped, as of 1963, to 23 percent. If we had today the share we had ten years ago, it would mean 750,000 more jobs, directly and indirectly, for American workers. Developments in other countries make it unreasonable to expect that we could have maintained that unusually high 1953 position. But this illustrates how directly export trade translates into jobs for American workers.

President Kennedy put the whole matter bluntly and completely when he proposed the Trade Expansion Act.

> If we cannot obtain new bargaining power to open up overseas markets, our export industries will wither—and American labor will lose jobs. If American businessmen cannot compete from here for the growing purchasing power of the European Common Market, many more will build their plants over there—and American labor will lose jobs. If we cannot find expanding outlets for the goods of an expanding economy, this nation's growth will be stifled—and American labor will lose jobs.
>
> In short, we are confronted with a very basic decision: Are we going to export our goods and crops—or are we going to export our capital and our job opportunities? Are we going to be the free world's greatest merchant trader—or merely its temporarily wealthiest banker?

The other side of this picture, the effects of *imports* on the employment situation, is harder to set out precisely. For example, some imports do not compete at all with United States products. We suffer no job loss at all from imports such as coffee and tin which we do not produce at all, or from imports such as newsprint which we do not produce in sufficient quantities to meet domestic needs.

It is clear from all the available evidence that many more job opportunities are created by exports than are lost to imports. It is likewise clear that trying to "protect" a job behind a tariff wall is exactly like trying to protect a job behind a "make-work" rule. High tariff "protectionism" and "featherbedding" come down to the same thing, which is giving artificial respiration to a job that is economically dead and making the consumer pay the price for it.

The soundest rule for foreign trade is in the old football maxim that the best defense is a good offense, which means concentrating on increasing exports instead of on stopping imports.

Why, then, is there any question about this policy? Partly because of inertia intensified by failure to recognize the change that has taken place in international trade; partly because of fear that we can no longer meet free competition in world markets because of our wage and price policies; and partly because of the very real fact that some segments of the economy have been injured in the past by import competition or fear that they would be exposed to such injury in the future.

Arthur Goldberg, when he was Secretary of Labor, pointed out the "false generality" of saying that high American wages and prices are responsible for "pricing ourselves out of" world markets.

> We are not being priced out of markets, as our balance of trade demonstrates. Our exports are concentrated in those very industries, such as machinery and coal mining, where wage levels are high by our own standards. High wage industries are usually efficient, well-managed, with skilled work forces. They are also the industries that survive and succeed in foreign markets.

The important labor cost figures for international trade purposes are those for unit labor costs. These costs reflect the impact of productivity. This is one reason why many of our high wage industries, such as coal mining, have such a favorable export balance. Although their wage rates are high, their productivity is so great that their unit labor costs are lower than those in many countries which have lower wage rates.

The importance of productivity in international trade is underlined by the fact that between 1953 and 1959 wages paid to manufacturing employees increased less in the United States in percentage terms than in any other industrial country. However, during that same period there was a substantially greater percentage increase in labor productivity in most other industrial countries than in the United States. This at least contributed to a relative increase in U.S. export prices and to the decline in the United States' percentage of the world export market during that period.

A wage increase which necessitates a price increase that pushes a producer out of a foreign market usually means a loss of jobs; and in general, but with different effects in different cases, wage increases which exceed increases in productivity have this potential effect.

Restraint is called for by both American management and labor. But part of our answer to the wage-price question is that we can, by greater efficiency, neutralize the competitive effect of lower hourly wage rates in other countries. It is important, too, to realize that living standards, and hourly wages, have been increasing faster, at least on a percentage basis, in most industrial countries than in the United States. We can expect that as these countries' economies continue to grow and prosper and as they gain assurance of their international trade position, their wage rates will continue to approach ours.

A freer trade policy is essential to that expansion of the American economy which offers the only long-range promise of full employment in this country. We cannot afford to become a dumping ground for the world's produce, but we must remember that we sell more abroad than we buy, and that there are no one-way gates through tariff walls. If we insist on buying American, our foreign customers will see to it that we sell American, and this will mean fewer jobs for Americans, not more.

Beyond this there is a need to widen our horizons beyond our immediate assignments and to look and think about where we are going as a nation. We live in a troubled world, beset by great power struggles both ideological and political, a world where poverty, illiteracy, and hunger are all too prevalent. These are revolutionary times, when new countries, new peoples, are reaching out for recognition of their dignity and presence. Our own revolutionary experience and tradition most often provide the inspiration for these new nations. The example of our economic and political development stands as a beacon light for their aspirations.

We must—as we are doing to a degree—reach out our hands to the impoverished, the hungry, and the underprivileged of the world. This has always been the American way. It must always be. With changing times, our methods and approach to such assistance must also change. We do not want countries of the free world to slip behind a paper curtain of trade restrictions which we have helped staple together. As in the past we opened our gates to the tides of people from other lands who, in their turn, helped build our strength and greatness, so now we must open our gates to the products of the newly developing countries to help them build, with us, a strong and vigorous world dedicated to freedom and to the dignity of man. This we must do as a matter of conscience, consistent with the ideals we live by, and as a matter of national interest in a divided world.

In a healthy, expanding economy such as we must achieve, there will be no serious difficulties in absorbing a fair share of the output of the less developed nations. An expanding level of consumer demand will not only help absorb our jobless, but also permit us to accept and even require the products of these developing nations. Exports expansion is a key element in the efforts to help the emerging nations find markets for their products. As we export more, we can import more and thereby help meet the many-sided objectives of our national policy: the improvement of our balance of payments, to be sure, but equally our feeling for humanity, our dedication to freedom and peace, our commitment to expand job opportunities through promoting full employment.

The Commonwealth of Human Responsibility*

Today's commencement thoughts cannot be separate from those we have for a month now been prisoner to. Nor should they be. Commencement is a time for summing up an education, and you in this class have come at the end of your curriculum to know how much more learning is from events than from tomes or teachers.

You had narrowed the ultimate issues down: to whether the ideas of love and reason are valid; whether there is any truth except in a laboratory; whether the individual can be an architect of meaningful purpose or is, in fact, assigned the part of pawn or puppet in a senseless drama of accident; whether freedom is too fragile for common use. But these were abstract issues.

Then suddenly, in a mad, macabre moment of history, they became starkly real. A single, searing event put to acid test the truth or half-truth, the meaning or unmeaning, the sense or sentiment, of the ideas and ideals you had been sixteen years constructing.

The immediate response for many of you was despair, even malediction. How can love prevail when hate can arm itself from a mail-order catalogue? What relevance has rea-

* University of Michigan Commencement Exercises, Ann Arbor, Michigan, December 19, 1963.

son when antireason degenerates to lunacy? If freedom depends on responsibility and restraint, is freedom better than farce when there is even one to use freedom's license for anarchy? It was easiest in that moment of untruth to say that if this can happen, if the worst of men can destroy the finest of men, if a single demented creature, fed on the hate and ignorance of a few, can despoil the work of millions, demean a nation in her own eyes and in the eyes of the world, then there is no pattern, no basis for believing in anything.

That first reaction was wrong. It was the product, largely, of self-pity. It is hard sometimes to have to live history.

To feel still, even after four healing weeks, a sense of incomparable, irreparable loss is to realize at the same time the lessons that have been offered any who will read them.

There is the lesson again of how infinite is the human capacity for meeting the onslaught of seemingly overpowering circumstance. We saw a nation's shattered faith in itself restored: by two women who had given that nation a son and a husband and who asserted silently now the quiet dignity of love; by a little girl's squeezing of her mother's hand and a little boy's unknowing salute; by the leaders of the world walking humbly behind a caisson to assert the elemental brotherhood which binds people closer than nations; by a new President affirming in resolute action and authentic statement the permanence of America's articles of faith and the continuity of democracy's purpose.

There is, too, a new measure of the important and the unimportant, of what matters and what doesn't matter. To have been part of tragedy, to have been hurt this much, is to feel a contempt for the insignificant. Marya Mannes has said, better: "A love, a grief, a loss so deep and wide [has] left no room . . . at all inside for what was sometimes harbored: little, mean, corroding thoughts . . . the sneer . . . the base untruth." More than before, and hopefully a working majority, will insist now that the questions before the nation be faced less in terms of narrow self-interest and more in terms of right and wrong, of truth and untruth.

There has been, most significantly of all, a new confrontation with the essential question of society's meaning: how far the human act and condition are influenced by membership in the commonwealth of man or how far they remain essentially a matter of individually inspired responsibility and irresponsibility.

This issue has been raised in terms of whether that incomprehensibly maniacal act in Dallas was traceable to a tragic flaw entirely inside one criminally maverick man or rather to what the forces of circumstance had done to twist his mind and make it the witless and unwitting tool of the merchants and mongers of hate and bigotry. Due process of reason permits as yet, on evidence so far at hand, no firm answer to that question. But when this is what those others sought, there is only secondary importance in whether their fulminations were a proximate cause of what happened in this particular instance.

The broader question is, however, infinitely important. For it is to the extent that what happens within a single human frame is the shared responsibility of the society as a whole that living and working have any meaning and purpose beyond satisfying the loneliest selfishness.

If years permit my commending any view to you, it is that the question is not what man *can* do in the improvement of the human estate, but what he *will* do, and that cynicism about this is made up mostly of ignorance, selfishness, or intellectual cowardice.

How far this is true as a matter of physiology I have no way of knowing, except that the number of pieces that have been added to the jigsaw puzzles of both birth and death just while I have been watching it make me think both puzzles may eventually be completed, and that there may not be so many pieces missing after all. Such a view is not heresy, but the highest faith.

I am thinking, however, not of what happens to the individual's physical tissue, but of what he becomes and does as a participating member of the society and the economy.

How can it be—whose fault is it—that there is today nothing for four million people to do in the midst of the most successful economic experiment in the history of society's development?

One view is that this failure is their own fault. That view, interestingly enough, is expressed in the same quarters, editorially, politically, and conversationally, where the position is taken most strongly that Lee Harvey Oswald was simply a throwback, and that the circumstances of his time and place are irrelevant. Another view of the unemployment situation is that there is nothing that can be done about it, or at least that needs to be done.

The theme, or thread, for the thoughts I shall try to leave with you today is that the current waste of human capacity in this country is very largely the consequence of public, not individual, fault, and that it is completely curable by common consent.

There is only a little oversimplification in identifying five causes of unemployment: taxes, inadequate education, poverty, racial prejudice, and careless automation. The first of these presents a separate problem; the others are closely interrelated.

Although the matter of taxes is of primary importance, it is enough to note here the error of trying to push an economy at a faster and faster rate, but with the brakes on. The tax cut will mean that the brakes will be taken off, releasing consumer purchasing power and increasing incentives to production to the extent required to bring the rate of job growth in this country back in rhythm with the growth rate in the population and the work force.

So far as the other, so-called "structural," aspects of unemployment are concerned, the dominant characteristic is inadequate education. The school system is no longer preparing enough people for the jobs that need to be done. The job needs have changed; the educational system hasn't. There are no longer enough unskilled jobs to take up the schools' failures. The usual price of a lack of education used to be commitment to common labor; now the price is frequently unemployment. There probably won't be full employment until we make education our No. 1 industry.

Most lack of education is related, not to stupidity, which is a more personal matter, but to poverty, which is not. We think of poverty as a result of unemployment. It is equally, perhaps more, a cause of unemployment, for the poor are today the parents of a new generation of inadequately motivated and inadequately educated boys and girls. A recent study disclosed that more than half of the men now between the ages of thirty-five and forty-four who failed to finish high school are sons of men who did not complete elementary school. Lack of education is directly related to unemployment; the unemployment rate for those with less than five years of school is seven and a half times that for those who completed college.

More and more we realize how much of unemployment is inherited, not through the physical genes but through the social genes of slums, broken families, and inadequate schools.

It hasn't been popular to talk about poverty in America. Yet at a time when the Gross National Product increases by thirty billion dollars in a single year but leaves thirty million Americans in families with annual incomes of less than $3,000, there is reason to recall Pericles saying almost 2,400 years ago: "Wealth we employ more for use than for show, and place the real disgrace of poverty not in owning to the fact but in declining the struggle against it." That was said, ironically, in what proved to be the first year of the decline of Athens' Golden Age. That there will be a more favorable turn of history this time is presaged in the fact that President Kennedy called as almost his last act, and President Johnson as almost his first, for a war on poverty. As long as millions of Americans are impoverished in spirit as well as in body, as long as millions of Americans lack the rudiments of an education, we make a mockery of the high ideals of the American tradition.

The relevance of racial discrimination to unemployment is written in the figures which show its incidence as more than twice as high among nonwhite as whites.

This year 1963 has seen the substantial winning of the hundred-year war against racial discrimination, but only the start of the necessary war now against racial disadvantage. This is the fallout problem from that other war. We have established the right to equal opportunity, but now we must guarantee the right to be ready, for opportunity is a delusion if it means only that a person not prepared for it is given the same offer as the person who is prepared.

There is recognition now that color marks neither capacity nor incapacity within the individual. But it is the responsibility of the commonwealth to compensate for a century of its own blindness to this fact. The plain truth of it is that a child born into a Negro family which carries the scars of a century of discrimination is not created equal to the child born into a family which has not been so marked and stunted. Ours is the larger responsibility to see to it that men who are not created equal are given the opportunity to achieve equality.

The remaining factor in the employment equation is this development referred to, loosely, as automation.

To some, "automation" is only a new name for a continuing process of man's mastery over technology that began when he attached a stone to the end of a club. And there has been, surely, ever since that time, a persistent ambivalence about whether this process has been a good idea or a bad one.

When the Don Quixote of Cervantes' imagination tilted at windmills in the seventeenth century, he was not applauded for his hostile gesture at a potential evil, but was ridiculed rather for lashing out at a harmless thing. Nor did the folk singer weep when Casey Jones was killed by his steam locomotive, for Casey loved his engine as an extension of his own manliness, and did not resent it as a competitor. His legend was one of triumph, for he died with the throttle in his hand. But in the main, our literature, our folklore, our art and philosophy have reflected a deep concern about the relationship of men and machines.

More characteristic than Casey Jones was "The Ballad of John Henry," which set an attitude of hostility to machinery that became a basic theme of American folk songs:

> John Henry said to his captain,
> A man ain't nothing but a man.
> An' before I'll let your steam drill beat me down,
> I'll die with the hammer in my hand.

Diego Rivera's oils are of machines that degrade and devour mankind. Rousseau and Thoreau planted the roots of antitechnology deep into our culture, with a pastoral negativism not unrelated to what you have more recently read in the literature of the Beat Generation.

It was Rudyard Kipling's couplet:

> What I ha' seen since ocean steam began
> Leaves me na doot for the machine: but what about the man?

And there was Ralph Waldo Emerson's poignant cry:

> Things are in the saddle and ride mankind.

The citizens of Samuel Butler's fictitious land of Erewhon destroyed all their machines, because a philosopher pointed out that the machines were improving faster than the men, and might eventually take over.

Yesterday's fiction finds its parallel in today's fact. A century which dawned on an industrial revolution that saw men concerned about becoming slaves has reached its high noon in a revolution of technology haunted rather by the specter of men's becoming robots.

Ten employees man a machine that makes automobile motor blocks four hundred men worked on ten years ago. Fourteen operators attend the glass-blowing machines that make 90 percent of all the glass light bulbs produced in this country. A machine translates an issue of *Pravda* into English in a half-hour. Another traces precedents in the law library. At Cal Tech, a computer reports at the end of three hours the results of eighty million calculations required to trace the evolution of the sun over its 4.5-billion-year lifetime.

Among the more athletic set, one machine plays now an excellent game of checkers, another a good game of chess except for the end play, and a third a relatively good hand of bridge. And there was last month's report even of cybernetic sacrilege—the Scottish computer that has proved that St. Paul was the author of only five of the fourteen epistles attributed to him in the New Testament.

Any philosophy or policy about automation must necessarily start from clear recognition that technological advance is not only inexorable, but is essential to the maintenance and elevation of the standard of living. Full employment in this country is completely dependent on our being more efficient producers than our competitors in a world where the competition is tougher every day.

It is equally clear that the prevalent myths about automation are narcotics dulling the national sensivity to the necessity of asserting men's mastery over machines.

The myth that automation is only a new stage in an old process is akin to the thinking that splitting the atom represented only an evolutionary development in the dynamics of war, a projection of the first use of the crossbow or the Trojan horse.

The comforting myth that we can always pull the plug of a machine out of the wall disregards the fact that we won't. And the companion suggestion that "Nothing comes out of machines except what men put into them" disregards the fact that this is probably no more true now of some machines than of some men.

The most dangerous myth, in immediate terms, is that machines produce as many jobs for men as they destroy and therefore represent no threat to workers. This is a half-truth, and therefore a half-lie. The truth is that machines *permit* the extension of men's work activities. The implied lie is that this will happen automatically or without the exercise of full human responsibility.

The jobs the machines create, furthermore, are usually for different people from those they displace. This doesn't matter if labor is viewed as a commodity. What it means, however, in more understanding terms is that the bargain a machine strikes with a man is that it takes one job and offers in return another—stripped of the worker's seniority, accrued vacation benefits, pension rights, and the value of the skill he had spent a lifetime developing.

The answers are not to smash the machines. They are to recognize that the individual versus the machine is as unfair a match today as the individual versus the corporation was in the last century, and that advancing technology requires the exercise of collective—public and private—responsibility for its effects and collective measures to carry out this responsibility.

A full employment policy must contain two elements, both of which are clearer for the kind of thinking that has characterized these last four weeks.

One of these elements is a renewed commitment to the idea of *full* employment, as a matter of human right.

A man replaced by a machine is entitled, assuming the exercise of full responsibility on his part, to another job either in the same enterprise or elsewhere, without reduction in earnings or loss of benefits and with full training provided if new skills are required.

This is easy to say, and hard to implement. It requires a revision of managerial policy, the relaxation of union restraints, a different collective bargaining attitude, a more enlightened vocational education training policy in the schools, a great deal more higher education, and probably an enlarged public retraining program. The rate of technological development will be greatly increased as provision is made for the recognition and protection of the individual, human interests which are affected by it.

There are those, and too many, whose sensitivities about the inhumanity of unemployment are dulled by the realization that it keeps wages down. There are others, and too many, whose tolerance for unemployment is increased by the realization that it does discourage inflation. There are far too many, themselves employed, who never develop much concern about those who are not. So there has been over 5 percent unemployment—which means four million people—in this country now for over six years.

If there were as much public emphasis on balancing the manpower budget as there is on balancing the economic budget, as much editorial concern about unemployment as there is about the dollar balance, we would be better able to accomplish *all* of our purposes. Democracy works well enough in this country that the priorities in people's minds do get translated into national policy.

The other essential element in a full employment policy is the recognition that its victims are for the most part casualties not of their own fault but of circumstance outside their control.

There are those, and too many, who seek balm for their conscience about unemployment in the conclusion that it is a state most of the unemployed deserve, or even prefer. This is callous, cruel untruth. The fairest conclusion from the studies and evidence now available is that probably about one person in two hundred, or perhaps three hundred, has some flaw within him that condemns him to dependence. This would be one-half of one percent, perhaps, of the work force. All the rest have the potential to work meaningfully.

Make no assumption that the boy who drops out of school and moves on then to unemployment, juvenile delinquency, or worse acts free of his environmental circumstance. If this graduating class is typical, eight out of ten of you, according to a recent study, are the sons or daughters of parents who attended college. By contrast, we interviewed last month in New York a group of 2,500 boys about your age, most of them "dropouts," who are already having a hard time of it. It turns out that 70 percent of their fathers didn't get beyond the eighth grade.

Recognize, similarly, that the ending of racial discrimination in employment is only half of that battle. The 20 percent unemployment rate existing today among younger Negroes looking for work represents in large part the fact that because there *was* discrimination a good many of this 20 percent group never developed the motivation to get a good education.

Our shared hope, the commonest hope in America today, is to find how to keep the murder of John Kennedy from going down in history as a brutal irrelevancy. Others, seeking to serve this same hope, see in that assassination principally the exposure of fundamentally deep weaknesses in American life. But fear, hate, bigotry, vituperation, murder—these are not our characteristics, and no ugly minority or madman will make them so. The central point seems to me only a little, but essentially, different. It is that whatever there is of individual human fault or failure or achievement is part of the common responsibility. Surely we want it that way, so that we can find the measure of our meaning and the fulfillment of our purpose not in a mirror but in other people's lives.

The other element of relevancy I can sense is the strengthening of purpose to pursue the issues of the day not in terms of a clash between political ideologies, but in terms of the balance between moral opposites. It is on the battle fronts between hate and love, vulgarity and decency, deceit and honor, fear and courage that you get a sense of what life is all about, for life is essentially a moral struggle.

So shall we seek, each in our own way, to find the meaning we know is in the eternal flame that will henceforth light our paths from a hillside above the Potomac.

VII

THE LANTERN LIGHT OF FAITH*

I SEE THE FUTURE more clearly in the soft lantern light of faith than in the glaring headlight of reason.

Eternity has already shrunk, in the illumination of logic, to a matter of minutes: that little time that can run while man lives a single spark away from ultimate destruction, his knowledge of power daily outstripping his wisdom about its use, with more and more of democracy's decision-makers knowing less and less of what they are deciding.

To care about the future only as it will see the ascendancy of human over material values is to watch with a fascination that fights against fear a generation of machines maturing as no generation of human beings ever has, so that any moment now some clanking robot will pull itself erect and announce: "*Cogito, ergo sum.*"

We take, nevertheless, the brief against that kind of reason, the brief for faith and for the future.

Children of unfathomable mystery, surrounded still by secrets that dwarf to insignificance what is so far known,

* Fiftieth Anniversary Banquet of the *New Republic,* Washington, D.C., March 5, 1964.

we have no basis, unless the premise be taken as itself the conclusion, for asserting that only what can be proved is true.

The only dangers, except for cataclysmic accident, are that we will build our syllogisms too much on experience, too little on vision; that we will forget that "The inevitable is only what we don't resist" and the unattainable only what we don't attempt; that we will stumble and fall on the sword of our own stupidity.

It is not the stupidity of the ignorant that threatens so much as the stupidity of the successful, who seek to protect their petty conceits behind Maginot lines of race or religion or geography, content with the little innovations of their own dubious piety, fighting change because the status quo has been good to them. The divine right of the successful is as false a notion as the divine right of kings.

We look ahead knowing the future is still infinite if we will stretch our minds far enough and fast enough to keep ideas abreast of ideals; if we will reassess, under technology's pressure, the revolutionary new relationship between war and peace and between work and leisure; if we will seize the sense of the future that will let us stand on a clear night and look at a heaven full of more stars than the number of all the men and women who have ever lived, and realize that those stars are now very close to our reach and are part of our children's future.

If we are because we think, we will be because we believe —even if only in the Grand Mystery of it all, and that it is worth the eternal quest.

INDEX

ABOUT THE AUTHOR

W. Willard Wirtz was appointed Secretary of Labor by President John F. Kennedy on August 30, 1962, confirmed by the Senate without hearings on September 20, and sworn into office at the White House on September 25.

Secretary Wirtz served as Under Secretary of Labor during the first twenty months of President Kennedy's Administration. From 1955 to 1961 he was engaged in the private practice of law with the firm of Stevenson, Rifkind & Wirtz in Chicago.

He was chairman of the National Wage Stabilization Board in 1946, general counsel and public member of the War Labor Board from 1943 to 1945, and assistant general counsel of the Board of Economic Warfare in 1942 and 1943.

Mr. Wirtz was for many years a teacher of law, first at the University of Iowa and then, from 1939 to 1941 and again from 1947 to 1961, at Northwestern University. He was also an active labor arbitrator during this period.

Mr. Wirtz was born in De Kalb, Illinois. He attended Northern Illinois University, the University of California in Berkeley, and is a graduate of Beloit College, in Beloit, Wisconsin. He received his law degree from the Harvard Law School.